Where did I go wrong
A Mother's Story

Where did I go wrong?

A Mother's Story

Sarah Speake

Sands
Stillbirth & neonatal death charity

Published by Bosun-Publications
Terminal House
Station Approach
Shepperton on Thames
TW17 8AS

Tel: 01932 242436

First published in Great Britain in 2007
by Bosun-Publications on behalf of
Sands, the stillbirth & neonatal death charity
28 Portland Place
London W1B 1LY

Tel: 020 7436 7940
Helpline: 020 7436 5881
Email: support@uk-sands.org
Website: www.uk-sands.org

ISBN: 09554243-7-2
ISBN: 978-0-9554243-7-3

Where did I go wrong - A Mother's story. Copyright © 2007 Sarah Speake

A CIP catalogue record for this book is available from the British Library.
Typeset in 12pt Minion
Printed in England by
Cpod, Trowbridge, Wiltshire

Book design and production by
FW Barter ARCA
Bosun-Publications
Email: fbarter@bosunpress.com

Contents

For our precious Amélie
and all the other special babies like her.

Foreword

I DECIDED TO WRITE this book the first day I was at my childhood home in Scotland, two days after our precious daughter Amélie died, for a number of reasons: I wanted to get every detail of her little life down on paper, so I never forget the intensity of emotions during her 11 days with us, and in some way to start sharing my true feelings with the rest of the world to help others understand.

It's never easy to know how to help, or the right thing to say or do, but I hope our journey enables other parents in our situation to realise that their utter despair, guilt and sorrow are perfectly normal, that it will get better, and for friends and family to understand the importance of support, friendship and love.

The number of letters and cards that have been sent to us already has been overwhelming, and a reflection of the friendships we will never lose but will now appreciate and treasure even more.

The medical profession will never get it completely right for every couple whose child is cruelly and inexplicably taken away from them, but the words, respect and care given to us remain etched in our memories forever............

Sarah Speake, March 24th, 2005
(The day after Amélie's funeral)

To dearest Amélie Charlotte
our beautiful grand-daughter
who will always have a
special place in our hearts and in our lives.
With lots of love
and big big hugs
from Nonna and JB

xxxx

Part One

It Wasn't Supposed To Be Like This

I had it all planned perfectly.

I GOT PREGNANT ON honeymoon (I haven't used the phrase "fell pregnant" as it's such a ridiculous notion and conjures up some very peculiar images in my head), despite or possibly because of, genuinely believing it would take months if not years. Either way, Martin and I were determined not to let the "trying" take over our lives, having seen the horrendous strain it put on friends' relationships, where it became the all-encompassing focus of their lives. So we just carried on as normal – both working full-time, exercising, socialising, travelling and generally enjoying life as a newly-married couple.

And then it started……………….. waves of nauseous light-headedness, hot flushes, slightly greasier skin than normal and just permanently feeling a bit odd. I've never been so amazed and overjoyed as the day I found out I was pregnant, but in my state of utter disbelief bought an additional 2 pregnancy tests "just to be sure". For such a major event, the complication in my over-excited state of deciphering blue lines was too much like hard work, so I opted for the digital variety that simply state "pregnant" or "not pregnant" to alleviate any confusion. Having always been a hoarder of significant cards, letters and presents, I do of course still have the test squirreled away in a special place.

So I'd joined the club of secret-carriers, and spent hours searching for the tell-tale signs I thought must be so obvious about me to other people – starry gazing into space, the wry smile, the hand on the invisible bump, and the adoration of all little people who looked even vaguely cute. I've always loved babies and kids, so the thought of having my own was a very special and, in my mind, miraculous concept.

However, throwing up on the tube into one of the many aeroplane sick bags I'd collected for my gorgeous car-sick prone nephew Olly was a really unpleasant and embarrassing experience, and doing major client presentations a serious challenge whilst feeling so permanently sick. Apart from the first four months of feeling absolutely rancid though, I felt fantastic during the rest of my pregnancy.

We found out we were having a girl at my 20 week scan and decided to call her Amélie Charlotte, but to keep her name to ourselves (any close girlfriends of mine will chuckle at this, as I did let slip to a couple of them – partly to ensure none of them stole it!).

"Let the planning commence"............................ we went to the Baby Show to test drive buggies on the pram and pushchair assault course, I had endless conversations with friends as to the merits of varying brands of breast pump, breast pads, baby clothes, cots, mattresses, maternity belts, car seats, maternity clothes, baby clothes, muslins, dummies, types of labour, pain relief etc. etc. etc. etc. etc. and of course everyone has an opinion!

Our little lady developed her own routine, kicking and wriggling at such exact times of the day I could have set my watch by it, and I found comfort in the fact that everything was obviously going so well. I had endless energy, was proud of my ever-expanding bump, and had bought or borrowed everything we needed to cater for the arrival of our Amélie.

I was in countdown mode, very much looking forward to meeting the little girl who squirmed around so regularly inside me, and had decided to take a week's holiday while Martin, the rest of my family and my best friend Pam went off on our annual ski trip to Avoriaz the first week of March.

Funnily enough, I had it all planned perfectly........

I'd drop Martin off at Gatwick so I could wave them all off, then spend a few hours on my own before the Arthurs arrived to spend the night with me in Chiswick. The plan was then to travel up to the Wirral with them the following day, via their friend Annie's near Stratford for lunch. Monday meant lunch with my great aunt Phyllis in Manchester to show her our wedding album, then back to London on Tuesday. Wednesday was the day to meet my oldest friend Saz's newborn baby girl Summer (the little friend Amélie would grow up with as Saz and I had), and catch up with Emma that evening before chilling out on Thursday and seeing Bobby Thursday night.

Friday morning was going to be my lie-in (if one ignores the inevitable number of times I would have to get out of bed to go to the loo, with our little lady pressing on my bladder so much more), before setting off to spend the day and overnight at my friend Rayne's. Rayney had booked me in to have an antenatal massage and some pampering during the afternoon, which I was very much looking forward to, then my plan was to meander slowly back to London in time to pick the Avoriaz ski crew up from Gatwick after their week away. Mum and Dad were due to stay overnight on the Saturday so we could all spend the day together before they flew back to Edinburgh late, particularly as Dad hadn't seen me to stroke my bump since we were all together in Scotland for Hogmanay.

I'd very excitedly told my dearest "cloggie" friend Saskia all about these plans the previous weekend when she and I had enjoyed a girls weekend together, catching up on all our news, drinking bubbly, (a token small amount in my pregnant state) and planning our summer holiday together in France with her little lady Lieve, with whom Amélie would also grow up. I was looking forward to being able to eat paté, foie gras, pink meat and drink lots of good wine that I'd avoided whilst pregnant.

After a lovely Saturday evening with the Arthurs (Srirat and David being the parents of my Godson Max and his sister Madeleine), we all went off to bed with Amélie kicking away for her night-time routine as usual.

I couldn't feel her move on Sunday morning, but assumed it was because I was expanding on a daily basis and she was therefore running out of room. Somewhat spookily in hindsight, having overheard me wish my own mother the same and therefore assumed it was a happy general greeting in the same way "Happy Easter" or "Happy Birthday" are, Max and Madeleine spontaneously yelled "Happy Mothers' Day Sarah" – it certainly didn't turn out to be.

Lunch with Annie was lovely, but I was becoming increasingly concerned that my little lady wasn't doing her usual karate kid show. Annie gave me a signed copy of her book "Trade Secrets" – the idiots'guide bible to kids from conception to teens, and I looked forward to referring to it as Amélie grew and developed. Little did I think the first relevant chapter I would chose to read a mere 10 days later when the writing was on the wall would be that on child bereavement.

I was pleased when it went dark on the remainder of the journey up to the Wirral so that noone else in the car could see my tears of anxiety, and was glad of the distraction of car games designed to occupy the kids in the back – "Blue Cow" was a new one to me, although inevitably I can't remember how it goes, in the same way I can never remember the exact plots of films I've seen. Srirat had suggested if I were still concerned by the time we arrived at their house, she would drive me to the local 24 hour Walk-In Centre at the hospital to put my mind at rest.

When we arrived at the Arthurs', I lay down for half an hour on my side, which usually instigated an inner dance routine from Amélie, but still nothing. Srirat (Rat) and David were putting the kids to bed and, although I found comfort in the knowledge they were so closeby, I have never felt so scared or alone. Rat came in to check I was OK and I remember sobbing "I'm shitting myself".

Ever practical, I took my maternity notes to the Walk-In Centre, in my heart of hearts expecting and desperately hoping not to need them, but to be told all was well. I was glad Rat was with me when we arrived, as she had to explain the problem – I had lost the power of speech when the Scouse guy at the desk asked me why I needed to see a Doctor. The waiting room was full of people who looked ill. I just looked pregnant and upset, and tried to occupy my time looking through my maternity notes with Rat – we laughed nervously at the fact I'd put "No" to alcohol consumption at my Booking Visit at the hospital, but I was feeling so sick at that stage of my pregnancy I certainly wasn't up for my usual tipples of champagne or red wine.

When we walked through to the examination room, the nurse on duty asked which one of us was Sarah Speake – as Rat in her diminutive state comes up to my chest even with heels on and was definitely not 34 weeks pregnant, we later giggled at the fact that with our coats on the nurse couldn't tell the difference. It wasn't the first time Rat had resolutely declared "I think it's time for me to lose some weight".

After a quick phone call to the Maternity Unit, the 3 of us walked across the car park and were met by a lovely French midwife called Annie who got me to lie on a hospital bed. She explained she would examine me and listen for the heartbeat to check everything was normal, and while she got her equipment ready and I stripped off as requested, we chatted about Avoriaz and the fact that my pregnancy had gone swimmingly well, but that the lack of movement that day was the reason for my visit. I was relieved when she could hear a heartbeat through her ear trumpet, so decided that, as all was presumably well, there'd be no need to worry Martin so I'd tell him on his return from skiing.

Annie (the name of the day!) put me on a baby heart monitor round my stomach and said they'd monitor the baby's heartrate for half an hour – I assumed this was "just to be sure", so lay there calmly while Rat played Doctor and messed around with the ear trumpet.

My World Has Stopped

Babies' heartrates are supposed to be between 110 and 160 – Amélie's was consistently between 170 and 180 and Annie looked concerned.

Within 5 minutes, the room was full of consultants, anaesthetists, paediatric experts and Annie, and I was on the receiving end of the most disturbing simultaneous canonfire of questions imaginable: wherewereyousupposedtogivebirthareyouallergictoanythingwho'syourdoctorwhatkindofanaestheticwouldyoulike**we'vegottogetthisbabyoutnow**where'syourhusbandcanyousignthisconsentformareyouscaredofneedleswhat'syouraddressdoyou understandyouhavetohaveanemergencyCsectionnow**we'v egottogetthisbabyoutnow**pleasecanyoutakeallyourclothesandjewelleryoffpleaseputyourheelstogetherandspreadyourlegstogetthiscatheterin**we'vegottogetthisbabyoutnow**.................................

Rat was meanwhile on her mobile to Martin who was out with the rest of the Speake and McArdle crew in Avoriaz celebrating the first evening of their holiday saying "No Martin you don't understand, it's too late to talk to a Doctor, she's going into surgery NOW" and us losing the signal when she handed the phone over for me to speak to him directly. The same happened when she had my Dad on the phone, and I left them speaking as I was wheeled into theatre. Although very shaken, I knew what to expect from a C-section, having developed an addiction to baby programmes during my pregnancy, and almost laughed when they asked again how comfortable I felt having an epidural – I couldn't have cared less by that point in my newly-surreal world.

The green sheet went up and I imagined what was about to happen on the other side of it. My head felt very hot and I thought I was going to throw up as a result of the epidural – with Rat by my head on one side muttering about could I please not throw up over her, and Scouse Gary on my other side trying desperately to distract me, I almost felt back in control. "The next bit feels like they're rummaging around in your handbag" warning from Rat was a perfect description, although I was so numb from the epidural it certainly didn't hurt. Gary laughed when I said Martin was a Man U supporter, and responded cheerily "Tell 'im yer daughter's a Kopite". Having never been a great fan of football, I've since discovered that one end of the Liverpool stadium is called the Kop.

Sadly I was completely unaware of when Amélie was born, as she was lifeless and floppy and was speedily whizzed off to the "SCBU" – I later became all too familiar with the Special Care Baby Unit.

Gary asked "'ave yer gorra a name for yer daughter?". In the way only I can I said "Yes, Amélie Charlotte Tewkesbury – would you like me to spell that for you?". Even under the influence of the large amounts of drugs I'd been given, I knew it had to be right. However, his response pleased me enormously ...."Oh she can't 'ave yer 'usband's name in 'ere luv. She's gorra be under your name 'ere in 'ospital – 'e's nor 'ere is 'e?". And so her hospital tag reads Amélie Speake, D.O.B. 6/03/05.

I was stitched up and cleaned up by the green scrubs brigade and wheeled to the Recovery Room – shock and the fact I'd lost over a litre of blood in surgery led to my shaking uncontrollably for the duration. It was in that tiny room that I learned how to watch a monitor for signs of patient change – my own rather than my daughter's at that stage, as I had drips, catheter and blood pressure tubes attached to monitor any potential relapse.

I insisted on speaking to Mum, Dad and Martin directly, as I knew they'd worry if they hadn't spoken to me personally. Mum later didn't remember speaking with me at all and she was also so traumatised by what had happened to me that she had convinced herself that it was my life at risk rather then Amélie's by the time she arrived at Arrowe Park. I was shaking so much with shock that Rat had to hold the phone for me to speak into.

And I still hadn't met my daughter.

I tried to convince them all I had recovered sufficiently to be wheeled to the SCBU to meet her, but as I still couldn't move my legs after the epidural there wasn't much chance of that happening. A lovely member of staff , Matt (we later discovered his real name was Howard Jones, so I could fully understand his not using it – he didn't look anything like his namesake '80s popstar) popped in to say they were trying to get a line in through Amélie's tummy button "which is a tricky operation". A midwife (I think) also appeared at some point and said that they should be back to get me in "half an hour to an hour". Inevitably it turned into more like 2, and I thought about all the training sessions I've led over the years at work about Managing Expectations. Reality seemed a lifetime ago, but Rat kept distracting me by pressing the morphine "watch" on my wrist to give me another shot – "bloody good stuff this. I remember it well" she repeated at regular intervals. Of the pair of us, by that stage only she had been aware of the amount of blood I'd lost, and made me laugh by describing how she'd seen it dripping down the side of the operating table in theatre and was strangely worried that it might reach and therefore ruin her sheepskin boots. In an amusing twist of fate, she spilt pancake mix over them the following week so ruined them herself quite successfully anyway.

I took great comfort in the fact that Dad was en route from Scotland, that Martin knew our daughter was alive, and that he and Mum were arranging flights to get to Liverpool airport from Geneva as soon as possible. I then worked out it could only have been around 9pm that we'd initially arrived at the Walk-In Centre and Amélie was born at 10.15pm, so an emergency indeed.

I was eventually wheeled upstairs to Ward 52 to be put to bed and, as they had no side rooms available, was deposited in a room with two new mothers with their perfect new-born babies. I could hear them making their snuffly noises as they slept and felt very distressed that I didn't even know whether Amélie could snuffle. I heard Dad's footsteps around 3am. It was the best hug my Dad had ever given me, and I felt his pain shaking through my hospital gown.

I was pleased to be helped into a wheelchair so that

Dad, Rat and I could finally meet my precious girl.

SCBUs are notoriously hot, disconcerting places full of incubators, bleeping machines and very ill babies fighting for their lives. They fall into 2 main categories – premature and seriously sick, and when I saw our little girl for the first time it was obvious she was certainly not the former. They'd clearly got my dates wrong, so the first Estimated Due Date of 1/04/05 I was given was more likely to be the accurate one.

I loved her perfect naked body instantly, but was shocked by the number of tubes that had perforated her smooth skin. She was 6 hours old by the time I met her. She had swollen eyes, hands and feet and Martin's dimpled chin. It wasn't until about Day 4 I also noticed what enormous feet she had – Martin's a size 13. I'm not sure how long I sat by her incubator in my wheelchair that first night, but it was to become my new home for the next 11 days.

She was completely naked except for the little pink bonnet she had to wear to keep the ventilator tubes stable in her mouth – when we finally took it off it still had my blood on it, that will stay forever in her box of keepsakes.

Rat and Dad went back to the Arthurs so we could all get some sleep – I was exhausted, but read crappy women's magazines in some poor attempt to do something vaguely normal after my abnormal evening. I did eventually manage 2 hours, only to be woken by someone pulling back the curtains around my bed so I had a full frontal view of the woman in the bed opposite and her perfectly healthy baby in the "tray" beside her. I'd never felt so bitter and resentful, although she was a sweet woman who asked me later if she could get me anything as I was clearly in distress.

I plugged myself into my mini iPod so I could switch off from the intimate chats both my roommates were having with their new sources of love, and racked my brains as to why any of this nightmare had happened. Could I have done anything differently to affect the outcome?

Had the fact I'd rejoined my old gym and been swimming the previous evening somehow affected Amélie inside me? Was it the spag bol I'd defrosted for us to eat the night before? Should I have gone to the hospital earlier? Was it the car crash we'd had on our previous trip to the Wirral? Had I eaten anything I shouldn't have during my pregnancy? Had the fact I'd flown reasonably regularly altered anything? Was it all the champagne I drank on the flight back from honeymoon? Would she live? What if she were handicapped? What if it were all my fault..............

Where Did I Go Wrong?.....................

I'm not sure now where I was when Martin and Mum arrived, but everyone in the hospital seemed to know our story and asked how they'd managed to get flights. Mum had aged decades since I'd seen her at Gatwick 2 days previously.

Martin sobbed when he saw me and our daughter for the first time, and clearly felt awful that he hadn't been there the previous evening – sadly these things can't be planned for. A surge of love, despair and utter helplessness washed over me, as I was faced with my own and his sorrow that it had all gone so horribly wrong. Whatever the outcome though, being held in my husband's arms, I knew we'd get through it together.

In the SCBU, I dutifully showed Mum and Martin how to wash their hands in accordance with hospital regulations so they could touch The Little Lady through the portholes in her incubator. It had already become second nature to me, and I'd scrubbed my hands almost red raw by the time we eventually left Arrowe Park Hospital on St. Patrick's Day.

It's Amazing How the Body Recovers

Day 1 is a bit of a blur, but it was probably then that we met James Robertson (Associate Specialist, whatever the hell that means) for the first time, and Adrian Hughes (Consultant), both of whom became a constant source of hope and despair in their combined decades of expertise within the SCBU.

Mum and Martin had wept when they saw Amélie, but I'd already become accustomed to the shocked reactions having seen Dad weep painfully, which he eventually stopped on Day 3 (or at least in front of me, poor man). I also realised that for my parents this was double whammy, seeing their own daughter in so much mental pain and their little granddaughter fighting for her life.

I was so shattered that first day that I could barely keep my eyes open, but insisted, despite my 2 hours sleep and major surgery less than 12 hours previously, on keeping vigil at Amélie's incubatorside (according to James, as she was actually born at 36 weeks gestation by their reckoning, she was "a big bugger for an incubator"). I was relieved to discover my body had recovered sufficiently not to require a blood transfusion after all, but the midwives were keeping a very close on me indeed to ensure I was in no danger of having a relapse. I had to keep my morphine drip and DVT socks on though. And of course I didn't have any of my own clothes, as I'd only intended to stay on the Wirral for 2 days.

We were told that The Little Lady was very seriously ill indeed and that they'd pumped her full of phenobarbitone (known as "phenobarb" by those in the know, which we hurriedly became for all the wrong reasons), an anti-epileptic "flattener" drug that was meant to give the experts a clearer and less confusing picture of symptoms and therefore potential causes of our daughter's floppy state. The only parts of her that weren't floppy were her clenched little hands that were very swollen through the insertion of drips, and her not so little feet from having such regular heel pricks to take blood. The only thing that was clear at that stage was that, for some unknown reason, Amélie had been temporarily starved of oxygen in the womb, which had caused her resulting coma. I was desperate to see the colour of her eyes, but knew it was unlikely she would ever open them of her own accord.

Where **Did** I Go Wrong?...........................

That night we were moved to the Snowdrop Room, a lovely room full of pots of silk snowdrops, with an en-suite stereotypical hospital bathroom in which I vowed I would never actually bathe, and a kitchen so we could make our own food. It had a security code on the outside known only to hospital staff (we soon worked it out) and a sliding "Enter / Do Not Enter" sign that proved to be utterly futile as noone ever paid any attention to our outer requests for privacy and quiet. I pushed to the back of my mind the fact that it was the room designated to bereaved parents and had been funded by *Sands (Stillborn And Neonatal Death Charity)*, believing that Amélie would recover. Rat later told me when I first saw her I turned round to my father and said "It's OK. She's going to make it Dad". I couldn't ever stop believing.

I think I slept for about 3 hours that first proper night with Martin in the Snowdrop Room, but was in so much physical pain that every time I moved in my sleep as I normally would, I managed to wake myself up by moving in the wrong direction or by needing to go the loo, which I still couldn't do unaided – as one of the nurses later said to me "I reckon yer dignity falls out with the placenta". I failed then and still fail to understand why anyone (unless of course for medical reasons) would actually opt to have a C-section as it can be a temporarily physically crippling procedure, which means no driving or lifting anything vaguely heavy for at least 6 weeks. And for someone as fit and healthy as I'd been, it was unsettling to feel so physically incapable, and to know that, whenever I saw them next, I would be unable to pick up and cuddle my nephew and niece Olly and Rosie. I longed to pour my love to a child who could respond, and desperately hoped it would be my own.

On Day 2, my catheter was removed and due to the mental strain we were under there was a small part of me that quite fancied keeping it in so I didn't have to battle with getting in and out of my wheelchair to be helped on and off the loo to perform such a basic function that my daughter hadn't yet (and may never) master. But removed it was, along with my morphine watch, which Rat berated me for getting rid of – the midwives were also astounded at my request to only have paracetemol rather than any stronger type of pain relief, but my own wellbeing simply paled into insignificance in comparison to the grave concerns I had about Amélie's health and, physically at least, I was well on the road to recovery.

Her sodium levels were dangerously low, despite being on a drip which included some sodium, and we learned that the kidneys should filter and absorb sodium rather than peeing it out, which is what Amélie had started to do by about half way through Day 2. We began to dread those daily conversations with the consultants after they'd completed their rounds of the Neonatal Unit, unless of course she had improved overnight, in which case we would proudly report to them that she was responding to touch, had "opened her bowels"(later in the week) or indeed managed consistently higher "resps" (breathing on her own as well as just being reliant on the ventilator) – that parental pride will never leave us.

At some point during those first hazy 48 hours, we were told by James that if she were taken off the ventilator, she probably wouldn't survive and, in the unlikely event that she did, she would be severely handicapped. We were also given the option of giving her another chance on the ventilator if she stopped breathing once taken off it, or "letting her go". She fought against it though and seemed to improve.

Martin and I were told to take ourselves off to discuss "the options", and thankfully had both independently decided that we would love to be having a conversation about how to cope with her handicaps if she did survive, and that of course she deserved another chance back on the ventilator if it came to that. We could both see how such decision-making and the awful pressure of being asked to play God with one's own child could completely destroy relationships – had we felt differently, one would always blame the other person for having made the wrong decision.

James had also recommended we ensure any family members we wanted to meet her "got their arses up to the Wirral as soon as possible" and that being no use as they were so upset was "a crap excuse that they'd later regret" – his blunt Yorkshire approach was both appreciated and dreaded, as we knew he would tell us exactly as it was in each of our conversations in the Quiet Room. The implication that any family we wanted should meet her speedily as she probably wouldn't make it was a grim possibility I alternated between ignoring and numbly accepting throughout our time at Arrowe Park.

But then she appeared to improve – she moved her legs for the first time when Dad tickled her knees and her heartrate dropped to around the low 160s, so not far off the parameters for "normal" babies. She did go a rather strange orange colour through jaundice, so had 48 hours "under the sunlamp" – Rat amusingly said it made her even more of a local "Scally" now that she'd already opted for the tanning shop! "Like mother like daughter", I proudly sent my support network a text about my high maintenance little lady, who'd also started responding to my touch and loved the massages I'd decided to give her throughout the day.

I also clung on to the hope that, as James had seen babies recover after being in Amélie's state on two occasions in 15 years, our Little Lady would be the third instance and we would be able to take her home eventually.

I don't believe Amélie could ever hear at all, but when we were allowed to get her out of her incubator to cuddle her against our skin, her heartrate dropped to within not just normal but healthy baby levels, she relaxed, and the number of breaths she managed to take own her own without the ventilator increased.

I'll never forget the feel of her smooth skin against mine, or the strength of love when I could actually kiss her little face. We became hastily oblivious to all the tubes and only saw our daughter as she was – a perfect baby.

We Weren't Alone In Our Pain

With Mum and Dad there, I didn't want Amélie to be too crowded, so we split our time between her incubator and the Parents' Sitting Room. The number of No Smoking posters in that sitting room amused and astounded us, as had the outdoor "Patients Only Smoking Room" just outside the entrance to the Neonatal Unit – I had visions of my defence case for murdering one of the women who could barely walk after surgery being helped outside to "'ave a ciggie". Why should such unhealthy undeserving excuses for human beings deserve the miracle of parenthood?

The Sitting Room had no heating, and a rocking chair that my brother Duncan broke on arrival – he and my fabulous sister-in-law "Coolie" had arrived on Day 3 at lunchtime and visibly collapsed on seeing me in my new and therefore unfamiliar pyjamas and dressing gown (Rat had been on a spending spree in an attempt to make me feel vaguely normal). Their first words when I proudly introduced Amélie were "Oh Saz, she's perfect" – I knew she looked it on the outside, but had no idea as to the state of her inner imperfections and probably never would. They mastered the handwashing routine and Dunk made me laugh by saying he knew exactly how to wash his hands thoroughly after his time working with our uncle Dennis, who has his own vetinary practice in Denmark – I remembered us both giggling as kids at the image we had playfully conjured up of vets "putting their hands up cows' bottoms and pulling out a pint of milk" – it's funny what you think of in times of adversity.

Tears poured down their cheeks as their touched her phenomenally smooth skin. She had little blond hairs on her arms and legs. As parents themselves, I knew them to be imagining the hopelessness of our situation and how they'd feel if it were Olly or Rosie.

My mother- and brother-in-law Sylvia and Rob also arrived later that day and sobbed as they hugged me. They too uttered "She's beautiful and perfect" and were devastated at the cruelty of our tragedy. Both kept sneaking in to look at Amélie and promised not to talk so she could have some peace and quiet, and I felt incredibly proud that our daughter was such a little bundle of love for all who met her.

Mum, Dad, Sylvia, Dunk, Coolie, Rob all learned to look for the slightest signs of improvement and would excitedly report back at the tiniest flicker of more life. Although I was happy for them to stroke her skin initially during those first few days, I then became incredibly protective and only allowed Martin or I to touch her. I felt guilty for excluding our families that major privilege, but needed more than ever to bond with our daughter in any way we could.

As soon as we were able, Martin and I embarked on the nappy changing and cleaning her little mouth with sterile water and a cotton bud. Her mouth got quite dry or gunky with the permanent ventilator tube that forced her tongue to curl. It was still like that when she died.

At least she'd also been able to have my milk for the last few days of her life, albeit through a tube in her nose that we took turns in filling from a syringe. Our clever Little Lady was soon up to 9mls / hour, and the nurses syringed anything back from the tube they could at every feed to check the levels of stomach acid and whether she was therefore actually absorbing and digesting it properly. She was, so I was convinced that it was helping.

Being fed my milk also made the shape of her face change – the puffiness of her first three days had long since disappeared and she'd developed a longer face shape similar to my own. She was a perfect combination of the Speake and Tewkesbury genes. I'll never know where her button nose came from, but it was very cute.

I spent many hours during that first tortuous week thinking about my cousin Kate and her husband Ade, whose son Tom was also very seriously ill for the first year of his life and regularly stopped breathing. Although I wrote at the time, I realised how utterly inadequate my gesture had been. I'd like to see them when we get back to London.

It was only when everyone later left on Day 7 that I realised in hindsight the level of strength required to carry other people's grief. I was surviving on 3 hours sleep a night, a diet of Rice Krispies, Rat's homemade chicken soup, Jaffa cakes, chocolate fingers, bananas and endless cups of decaffeinated Earl Grey tea. I'd taken it very seriously when Annie (the name of the week!), the Feeding Advisor, had recommended I drink no more than 6 caffeinated cups of tea a day, so I'd reverted to my favourite decaff Earl Grey as I'd drunk throughout my pregnancy. I had thought Amélie would at least be used to it should she ever be able to fed my milk.

Rat, David, Mum, Dad, Dunk and Coolie would appear daily with clean clothes, home-made cooking and baking (that reminds me, I must get Rat to send the nurses her brownie recipe!) and allowed us some semblance of normality in a world where I had no fresh air, and where my daily route took me between the SCBU, Snowdrop Room and disabled shower – the only place I could have space without the threatening proximity of new mothers boring no particular chosen audience with the agonies of breastfeeding – they had NO idea how lucky they were.

Breast Is Best

Day 3 was the day I was first shown by Annie how to hand express the colostrum my body was of course producing – a minute amount initially that was put into a syringe and frozen with a sticker stating it was for Amélie Speake. I was later shown the designated freezer tray in which all my milk was being stored so that every time I expressed I could simply label each bottle correctly with the date and time and place it in order – freshest at the back. It keeps for 3 months at –21 degrees C. Mine was the only tray that was unnamed in the entire freezer – I put to the back of my mind that this was probably because it would end up in the Wirral Milk Bank rather than being fed to Amélie.

I dutifully hooked myself up to the double milk pump in the nursery every day from then on, and expressed like a Jersey cow. I proudly graduated from syringefuls of 0.5mls of colostrum to 90mls of breast milk within 2 days. Sometimes, my early morning expressing sessions in the milking parlour nursery were my one time alone for the day, and in those moments in that hot little room I both wept and smiled, knowing my Little Lady's "inc" was literally on the other side of the wall. As was the case upstairs with privacy in the Snowdrop Room, one poor nurse at 6am one morning forgot to check the "Vacant / Engaged" sign on the door and burst in talking to herself – she was far more embarrassed than I was and word soon got round the Unit that she'd walked in on my private pumping session. Even funnier was the day I emerged from the nursery with my father and brother in tow with their cups of tea to be met in the corridor by two sets of astounded parents who obviously came from less close and open families than my own.

I'd already decided by Day 4 to have the conversation with Annie about donating any spare milk to the Wirral Milk Bank, so had the relevant blood tests and filled out all the necessary forms. If Amélie died, I knew I'd be incapable of such practicalities at the time, yet desperately hoped that Annie would never have cause to use the milk for some other poor little mite who may need it.

I've always been mocked by friends and family for my anally retentive forward planning, but on this occasion I'm glad I did it.

Humour And Hugs

The colloquialism "'Scouse" is an abbreviation of the word "lobscouse", meaning "a stew or hash with vegetables or biscuit, a sea dish", presumably in reference to Liverpool's geographical position as a port. The resulting definition of "Scouse" is "a native of Liverpool: the northern English dialect spoken in and around Liverpool." I'm not sure whether the associated word "Scally" is a 21st century derivation of this, or comes from the word "scallywag" (both possible!), but either way the people we met during our stay at Arrowe Park, whether Scousers or scallywags, were a very eclectic and special bunch. I doubt I've ever met, or will ever meet in the future, a group of individuals with such a sense of caring warmth, love and compassion. And God did they make us laugh!

My first experience of their sense of humour was when I was whisked off to learn how to express milk more efficiently by a mad woman called Sue, who worked in the Neonatal Unit. She'd first met my family by walking into the Parents' Sitting Room to see me with my pyjama bottoms pulled down showing my parents how my scar was healing, so she set the scene for our relationship by insinuating that "folk like you lo'" were on a different planet. She dragged me off with a cheery "Cum on Daisy – let's sort yer ou'! I wan' at least a cuppla pints from yer!"

During the 11 days of our horrific ordeal with Amélie, we did manage to laugh uproariously, sometimes in nervous tension, and at other times because of something that seemed hilariously funny at the time.

Martin and I often switched on the television on returning to the Snowdrop Room for the night, usually exhausted mentally and physically and therefore in need of a distraction which required no mental effort from either of us. One evening there was a programme on about TV advertisements which have never actually been broadcast, having been banned by the Advertising Standards Authority. One of the ads showed a series of events involving a little girl: walking along with an ice cream cone and dropping it on the pavement; straining and failing to reach something that was just out of reach on a high cabinet to name a couple....... on realising each of these minor disasters, the little girl loudly declared "Bollocks", which literally had me clutching my newly-stitched stomach in the hope I wouldn't burst the surgeon's handiwork. It then transpired that during the filming, this little girl and her twin sister had been taught to say "Jackson Pollock", which when dubbed did of course look as if these innocent little girls were actually proclaiming such an inappropriate word. After wondering of course where the girls had picked up such an obscenity, at the end of the ad, we then saw the girls' father filling up with petrol at a petrol station, looking more closely at the pump and also loudly saying "Bollocks!".

It was a diesel car and an ad I will never forget...

I often wandered down to the SCBU in the middle of the night on my own to be with Amélie, on one occasion to be met with "Oh 'ere cums Lady Muck for 'er tea and toast!". The nurses working the night shift were a special breed unto themselves, and teased me mercilessly for being "The posh burd from London with a French name for 'er daughter". They were my saviours during the many hours of despair as I sat there cuddling my very sick Amélie. They hugged and held me, wound me up, fed and watered me, chatted or just left me in peace to treasure the quieter moments while the rest of the world slept.

Pauline, who also wrote a beautiful letter to us after Amélie died, told me one day (she knew me well enough by then) "yer look like a bag of shit" – and I did, but it made me laugh. They all got to know us both so well during our intense time at Arrowe Park that in anything other circumstances it would have been the start of many beautiful friendships. Sadly, our time together was born out of tragedy, although I do intend to keep in touch with some of our temporary saviours.

It was also Pauline who had me in hysterics to get me out of one of my more depressed moments by stating "Oooooh I gerrit now... the bunnies are 'cos you pair were at it like bunnies on honeymoon" in reference to the 3 little Easter bunnies in Amélie's cot and the fact I'd got pregnant so quickly. She also made me laugh by commenting on my new mother comedy chest, which admittedly did remind even me of a Kenny Everett sketch in which he'd donned a false chest with enormous breasts.

One morning when I went back up to the Snowdrop Room to wake Martin up, there was a local TV news bulletin about the plans to make Liverpool the first no smoking city in the UK – another instigator for me having to hold my stomach as I guffawed. I've never, (including my many trips to France, Spain and Italy where I didn't think it possible to smoke any more than the locals there did) come across so many people who epitomise unhealthy living. Almost all the other patients at Arrowe Park smoked – to the extent that vehement anti-smoker Martin was greeted with a look of astonishment when, on "health promotion day" in the hospital he was approached by one of the health visitors to talk about healthy living. It just seemed ironic and an insurmountable challenge.

Symbolism and Coincidences

One day I walked down to the SCBU to see our Little Lady wearing a gorgeous pink dress that one of the nurses had put her in during the night. It buttoned up the back, so that her arms could be put into it and the remainder of the dress could be tucked on either side of her and therefore not interfere with the many tubes keeping her alive. It made her look like a proper little baby girl and pushed me over the edge when I first saw her in it. That dress set the trend for the other mainly pink dresses Mum and Dad and Dunk and Coolie bought, so she had a different outfit on every day from then on.

By Day 7 I was completely mobile and wearing the flip flops and bright pink "Scally" tracksuit Saz had sent me. Mum got it wrong trying to search in her traumatised state for the word "Scally" and said "ooh you look like a real slaggy today", which caused great hilarity all round.

I've worn pink every day since she died.

Julie, the Paediatric Registrar, had just returned from 6 months maternity leave and was already ensconced in a deep conversation with Mum the first day I met her (although I'm not sure how much of the talking Julie herself was actually allowed to do). They'd already discovered that Julie had been at St. Andrews University at the same time I was, so we talked about the friends and places we had in common. It was a comfort to have that trusted connection, and Julie and I soon developed a bond.

Julie's first son, who is now a healthy 2 year old, had had significant health problems during the first few months of his life, and Julie and her husband had therefore experienced the agonising rollercoaster we too were being subjected to. Our situation clearly upset her, and I think our early morning Mummy conversations were probably as much of a tonic for her as for me.

The Registrar with whom Martin registered Amélie's birth and we later both registered her death had a daughter at St. Andrews who had studied Modern Languages and therefore spent a year out in Germany exactly as I had. I also found comfort in this odd connection.

And then there's the Marmite – you either love it or hate it. I've always loved it, and one morning sent Mum a text message at 06.01am to give her my daily update on the kind of night Amélie had had, whilst sitting back in bed temporarily, eating toast and Marmite. She switched her mobile on at exactly the time I sent my text and was also in bed eating toast and Marmite – weird.

My cousin Kate bought 2 trees to be planted in Tiny Toes part of Donkleywood in Northumberland in Amélie's memory. Our friends Lolo and Jeremy had also bought 2 trees to be planted in exactly the same wood as a wedding present for us last year. Spooky.

Mum gave Rat a book by Alice Thomas Ellis to say thank you for having so many of the Speake crew to stay. Not long after receiving this present, Rat picked out a couple of David's mother's old cookbooks – one of them a translation of a French cook book from 1967. Inside were a couple of newspaper cuttings with recipes, but on the other side of the recipe clipping was an article on Alice Thomas Ellis…. she had had seven children in total, but the clip mentioned she had also had a baby girl who only lived for 2 days. This particular coincidence, having since read the article in question, still gives me goose pimples, especially as I know noone in the Arthur household had opened the book for 8 years since David's mother died in 1997.

In some way I started looking for more coincidences in my bewildered and traumatised state, to the level where I genuinely believed the free book I'd been given with the last magazine I bought in the hospital was one of Annie's – I later discovered Rat had brought it into hospital for me and was somehow disappointed.

Coincidences appeared to occur more regularly, which I took great delight in, in the vague hope that they were somehow a good sign and that miraculously Amélie would wake up, recover and we could take her home in an ambulance with us to Chiswick where her things were waiting for her.

That day never came.

Medical Staff

The first thing they warned me about was the hospital food. As I never sampled anything other than the sandwiches, I never discovered for myself how bad it was. But we were left salads and brown bread after our initial protestations, and left little notes by a woman whose name I sadly can't remember, proudly stating the healthy options she'd wangled for us! Our Wirral support network was promptly issued with a list of things we felt like eating, so we had the luxury of home-made spaghetti bolognese, fresh salads, chicken broth etc. in the Snowdrop Room.

Whether the midwives, nurses, cleaners, lunch-providers, pain relief trolley wheelers on Ward 52 or any of the staff in the Neonatal Unit, they were all fabulous:

Adrian, with his daft socks and ties to entertain the kids in Paeds; James with his website *(www.yourchild-shealth.nhs.uk)*, books published, hatred of DIY and his wife's chicken and ham curry; Marcus, lover of his Mummy's socks and impatience at spending long car journeys with his 4 kids in the back; Kerry, who was almost pissed off to discover on taking my stitches out that I didn't have any stretch marks; Lynne encouraging her son to study by creating a special study area for him and who'd given us a surgical needle bucket to chill our champagne; Pauline, trying to get her husband Steve to share her enthusiasm for skiing and sharing my intolerance of bad grammar; Rachel – getting married towards the end of the year and excitedly planning it with her partner who also works in the care profession; Anne, who flew around super-efficiently multi-tasking in the SCBU; Lisa, whom I didn't get to know very well, but whose hugs were greatly appreciated when I fell apart; Cheryl who was trying to lose weight with Paul McKenna tapes; Janet, who seemed to have more health problems than most of the patients in the hospital put together; Brenda, who had been offered a job with the WHO and was daunted by the prospect of travelling down to London for the interview.....................

the one thing they all shared was how much they cared, which was evident.

It can't be easy showing empathy and compassion in some instances to parents who have actually caused their babies' severe health problems by taking crack or neglecting their health, as was the case with some of the poor mites in the SCBU while Amélie was there, – knowing inwardly that the start in life those poor babies had on leaving the hospital was a far cry from ideal, and yet outwardly showing no signs of judgement or morality and simply doing the absolute best for each of their little patients. The care I was given was also second-to-none, but for Amélie there was only so much they could do.

They couldn't make her breathe for herself.

She Made The Decision

St. Patrick's Day, Thursday March 17th 2005.

I'd had my usual Mummy time with Amélie between 6am and 8am and was feeling good about the day ahead. Her resps were better, so I pottered upstairs to wake Martin up and get bathed and dressed for the day. The sun was shining.

By the time we returned to the SCBU, she wasn't breathing at all on her own and, for the first time yet, however strange this might sound, she actually looked ill.

I got her out for a cuddle and Martin went off to log on and make some phone calls. I knew from the look on James' face when he asked where Martin was and how long he would be that the time had come to let her go.

That walk to the Quiet Room for our final crappy conversation with James and Lynne was the longest yet, past the outer nurseries in the Neonatal Unit with the parents and staff we knew so well.

"I take it from your facial expressions you know where we're at" were James' first words. I couldn't hold it together any longer and broke down. Lynne was fighting back the tears too.

We reiterated how thankful we were for their candour with us as Amélie's parents, commented on how ill she now looked and how aware we were of the breathing problem. "She's letting you know she's ready" – and we both felt she was. Too much of my milk was coming back into the syringe so she wasn't coping properly with being fed any more either.

I finally admitted to myself and everyone else in the room that I'd been using the evident phenobarb levels in her system as an excuse to buy myself more time with the Little Lady. More time was neither fair on Amélie nor an option.

Martin and I were left on our own in our rocked world to prepare ourselves for the worst day of our lives.

The sun was still shining.

Peaceful Passing

After our conversation with James and Lynne, Martin and I returned to the SCBU for our last cuddle each with Amélie. I did some filming and desperately tried to memorise every detail – how she looked, what the weather was like, the view from her window, what she was wearing, and achingly knowing we would watch the resulting DVD when she was dead. Nothing can describe that pain and despair.

I methodically cleared all her cards and little Emile and Rose box we'd kept her pink wardrobe in from the windowsill. Her name tags came too and, although tears streamed silently down my face as I started collecting what were soon to be become mementos, I had to do it myself. I even took the Cow & Gate jar of sterile water dated "Amélie 17/03/05" and ensured it went upright into the box so that none of it spilled.

I left Martin cuddling our precious daughter, cleared all our belongings from the lockers we'd used in the Parents' Sitting Room and went upstairs to prepare the Snowdrop Room and myself for our daughter's death.

A young couple and another mother were in the Sitting Room while I cleared our things – it was the only time anyone else had been in the space we'd monopolised for our own families, and the young couple with twins in the SCBU were also in tears holding one another. Martin and I had been with Amélie and ushered out of the SCBU as one of their twins had gone into what looked like cardiac arrest the day before. At least we knew with Amélie it would be quiet and private and not involve beeping machines, panic and drama.

It was surreal changing my top so that I looked nice for the photos I knew we would take of one another as Amélie died. I chose a white maternity top Pam had lent me to go with my new Next jeans and boots. It was important that I looked good for our little girl. I even put lipgloss on, and thought of my colleague and friend Lisa who's addicted to the stuff.

I moved all our clothes from the floor of the Snowdrop Room and shoved them in the wardrobe out of sight, put flowers on the windowsill with the framed photos behind the sofa, knowing that we'd soon be holding Amélie on that very sofa and wondering how long it would take for her to die in our room once the tubes were taken out.

I decided I wanted to see her in a white baby grow so I could hold her over my shoulder and feel like a normal Mummy, then when the room was ready walked back downstairs through the ward.

We'd have to plant snowdrops in her memory.

As I walked through Ward 52, I thought how recently it was that I'd been in that dreadful side room the first night, and how odd it was to be dressed in such normal clothes that I certainly didn't look like I'd just had a baby. In some way, I didn't feel like I had either, and wanted desperately to turn back the clock, have my big bump back and see my little karate kid kicking inside me.

Where Did I Go Wrong?..........................

Martin was still cuddling the Little Lady when I returned to the SCBU and I sat watching them. I didn't feel the need to cuddle her again downstairs, as I'd had many hours with her on my own during the long nights and knew I'd always want more time that no longer existed.

Lynne and James got her ready – it was the only time she was in a normal baby "tray", without any of the tubes, but with a mobile ventilator to ensure she didn't become distressed during the death march upstairs. I was pleased I'd insisted she have her umbilical tube taken out 2 days previously as it had almost completely healed by the time she was ready to go.

We walked a new route through the hospital, coming out by the Theatre I'd presumably been in for my emergency surgery. Another couple tried to get in the lift with us, but James asked them to get the next one. As I looked in the lift mirror, I actually looked the best I'd looked since arriving at this God awful place 11 days previously and thought how sad it was we hadn't even been there a fortnight – I don't know why but it seemed important.

Lynne was finding it as difficult as we were, but stayed professional to the end. Someone had opened the Snowdrop security door for us in preparation and everyone on Ward 52 had been pre-warned. I then remembered as they removed the mobile ventilator that when I'd been in The Room half an hour previously, one of the jolly Ward 52 staff who had some teeth missing had cried and said "I'm so, so sorry hon – there's nothing I can say or do to help" – and there wasn't.

James and Lynne explained that because Amélie's heart and lungs were strong and normal, "it could take some time", but none of us really knew whether she'd keep fighting as she had done, or give up quickly. True to form she kept fighting.

They left us on our own, our sad little family, and promised to return at regular intervals.

I felt her fill her nappy after about an hour, so decided

that was the time to change her and take off the floral dress from Dunk & Coolie to put her in something we, her parents, had chosen. I kept getting the sticky bits of the nappy the wrong way round in my traumatised state. Although she was already a very ill colour by then, I took some comfort in seeing her naked body on our white bed without the tubes. She looked perfect in the white baby grow, and we cuddled her over our shoulders. Lynne had given her a white knitted cardigan that she wore too. It still smells of her.

We took some beautiful photos of each other with Amélie and James took some of our little family on the required trips into our room to check how things were progressing. I didn't appreciate at the time how important those photographs would become.

Noone can ever take that precious time away from us, and in those two hours in the Snowdrop Room we held and kissed her, together and individually and watched her fade.

The sun was shining.

James came in again, felt her non-existent heartrate and said "Shall we say four o'clock?" – neither Martin nor I had any idea what time it was, nor that she'd finally gone, so both assumed he was agreeing the time for his next intrusion into our final space. Sadly, he was referring to her time of death.

Although to others it may sound crass, James' comment "although we prefer to do living well, we do dying well too" was absolutely true. The staff at Arrowe Park gave us and Amélie the peace, dignity and respect we needed. I'll never forget one of James' other many comments either: "Don't forget Amélie is and will always be your baby. We've just borrowed her." And they'd borrowed her beautifully.

Clearing The Room

We kissed her still perfect body Goodbye and agreed to keep her exactly as she was – not to have her hair washed and therefore be interfered with any more. I handed her over to James wrapped in a beautiful hand-knitted multi-coloured pastel blanket.

And that was it – our journey was over.

I don't remember how long Martin and I hugged and sobbed, but we'd cleared half the room and were drinking wine by the time James and Lynne reappeared. James told me to sit down, I guess in case I collapsed, but I'd been sitting down for two hours with our dying daughter so perched on the edge of the sofa as he and Lynne checked our plans and state of mind.

We'd decided to take her to Scotland. She didn't belong on the Wirral.

They both hugged us as they left. Lynne wept.

I wasn't ready to face anyone else by then, so sat on the edge of that sofa looking out into the world I was about to rejoin. It was surreal to think the people in their cars on the road outside were continuing as normal. Our lives would never be normal again.

I phoned Dad, who broke down, and I tried desperately to get hold of Dunk. He was on a train with a very bad mobile signal, so I phoned Coolie. She kept saying "Oh darling. Oh darling. I'm SO sorry." I knew she was, and knew that she was keeping it together for my sake but would howl privately in whichever room she'd hidden in at work to take my call.

Mum and David (soon to become the other name of the week!) arrived some time later. David didn't know what to say so just hugged me as he cleared our bags to take them to the car. Mum looked destroyed.

We got back to the Arthurs' house and I couldn't face going in yet, so sat outside with a very large glass of red wine. It was going dark. Max and Madeleine came out, looked at me sheepishly having been told and both gave me a big hug. I wondered what and how Olly would be told.

Martin walked around the garden on his mobile telling everyone else who needed to know then and I sat on the cold step, numb. It was a beautiful evening and the sky was full of bright stars. Eventually, it got so cold David lit a bonfire outside. Dad loves bonfires. Amélie would never have a chance to see or feel the heat from one.

I was persuaded to go in and eat, which was the last thing I felt like doing, but my food had already been cut up for me so I didn't even have to use a fork, which helped.

At some point during that dreadful hazy evening, Rat showed me how to use the breastpump I badly needed as my body thought my Little Lady was still alive and hungry. I had to use it for another 8 days before my body gravely admitted she'd gone.

Rat ran me a bath and she and Mum sat with me while I soaked in very hot water. My scar prompted a comparison between the three of us and Rat read to us both from a Nora Seton book that was already 3 weeks overdue at the library. It was a beautiful chapter and I took it to bed with me while Martin continued drinking with David downstairs. I'd planned to read it again in the bed on which I'd given my pregnant stomach a final chance to move less than a fortnight previously, but passed out through drunken exhaustion.

I knew we had to back at the hospital the next morning at 9am to sort out the necessary logistics and paperwork to take Amélie back to Scotland.

Red Tape and Cockups

The following morning I had to pour my expressed milk down the sink as my daughter's life had poured away the previous day. I had a headache, but deserved to feel far worse than I actually did – nervous energy and trauma count for a lot.

Martin was sick through shock and alcoholic over-indulgence that morning for the first time in our entire relationship, then we set off for the hospital. There were daffodils at the roadside and the sun was still shining.

As we got out of the car, Mum asked if she could see Amélie, but it was only appropriate that Martin and I were the last to see her, and it would have killed Mum had she seen the Little Lady dead rather than as we wanted her to be remembered. She was later glad of that decision. I'm glad too.

Even at times like that, people are kept waiting. We were pleased to see the familiar face of Sheila, one of the Neonatal Nurses, at the hospital's General Office. She explained that Adrian Hughes would be along shortly, of which we were both glad.

We wanted a plain white coffin to take her home in.

The woman from the General Office, yet another Lynne, explained that James had spoken with the Registrar – we had an appointment to register her death at either 10am or 12 that same day. Our conversation with Adrian, Sheila and Lynne didn't take very long, so we opted for 10am. Adrian wished us all the best and said they'd like to see us in 6 weeks as they normally would for local patients and we agreed that was a good idea. I was already thinking we could combine it with the trip to Scotland we'd planned with Amélie for early May. Except she wouldn't be with us now.

On the way out, we bumped into Sue, one of the other Neonatal staff who'd nicknamed me Daisy, who burst into tears when she saw us both and gave us each a huge hug. We touched a lot of people during our time at Arrowe Park.

We went off to Birkenhead Town Hall and of course Martin could navigate as he'd been there a mere four days previously to register Amélie's birth. I'm glad she was made official while she was still alive, and it was important that she was given her proper Tewkesbury name.

We went back to the hospital to check on the progress of Lynne's conversations with their contracted Funeral Director and agreed that we didn't want Amélie to be moved elsewhere from the hospital mortuary - even if there were building works going on outside. I suppose they were only trying to make it perfect and minimise our distress.

I spent the afternoon with Rat in the sunshine on the kids' trampoline and I probably drank about 2 bottles of rosé. We talked about Amélie, laughed at Rat having unexpectedly become my birthing partner and agreed it was a good idea to plant an Amélie garden wherever we could – she certainly deserved to have one in the Arthurs garden on the Wirral as well as those at home in Scotland and Chiswick.

Martin went off to the hospital on his own to sort the final paperwork and had a strange facial expression on his return.

The hospital had worked their magic and he had Amélie in the boot of the car.

I made him move the car into the shade and went to have a look at the coffin. It was perfect – white with brass handles and a plaque on the top for "Baby Amélie Speake / Tewkesbury". We all drank much more wine outside for the rest of the afternoon, then Rat and I retired to the bonfire to continue.

Mum had meanwhile spoken to our local Funeral Director David Lloyd, who had asked which paperwork we had. It transpired that we needed an "Out of England" certificate to take Amélie out of the country and that bodies should not actually be released for 4 days. So they'd cocked up, but I realised they were hardly likely to take our daughter away from us at that stage and "anyway the Coroner was going out that evening", which seemed remarkable. Martin went to his house to pick up the missing paperwork and I've never been so glad of a bureaucratic mistake in my entire life.

I somehow took comfort in having Amélie with us.

Dad arrived from Scotland to eat before turning round again to take us all home. He arrived at 9pm, so we left at half past.

The Journey Home

Dad drove as far as Southwaite Services. I never want to go there again, but we had to stop so that he and Mum could swap driving. We went in to use the loo, and I walked past a skinny pregnant schoolgirl who can't have been more than 15. It just didn't seem fair or right, but then nothing ever would again.

I've travelled that road so often, but never before has the journey seemed so long. Towards the end Mum was getting tired and talked incessantly in her nervous state – I can't remember any of her chosen topics.

Anticipation, I've discovered, is far worse than reality. I was dreading arriving at home and Dad, in the back of the car with me, sensed my unease so gripped my hand. I knew in the darkness that he was crying too.

I worried that Amélie would be rocked around in the boot as we drove up the bumpy potholey lane towards our drive so asked Mum to slow down. There was a tree on the back door step as we drove round to our own front door.

I asked Mum and Dad to wait elsewhere in the house, as it only seemed right that Martin and I took Amélie inside. I clutched her coffin and wanted her little body to be alive and well so badly. Martin made me move away, otherwise he knew I would have slept with her in my arms. I could picture my baby in her little white babygrow within it.

There *was* a tree on the back doorstep and a card in the kitchen that someone had brought inside. The tree was called "Prunus Princess", which flowers white blossom in early March that turns pink – a perfect present from an unknown friend that made us weep.

I should have known it was from Marge, my "other mother" who'd known me since I was three, on the day her daughter Saz and I met at nursery school.

We went to bed at 3am and I woke up 4 hours later to go downstairs and see Amélie as I had every time I'd woken up over the previous 11 days. I knew we only had a few final hours with her at home until David Lloyd came at 1pm to take her away.

Saying Goodbye

Never in a million years did I ever think I may have to plan my own child's funeral, but I knew it had to be perfect like she was. David, an old schoolfriend of mine, who was also the Funeral Director for my Grandpa's cremation, visited on Saturday March 19th to discuss the details. The pain on his face when I opened the door was visible, and he seemed to have aged even more than I felt I had as a result of our news.

We sat in the lounge, with Mum and Dad sitting helplessly in the kitchen imagining the painful conversation happening on the other side of the wall. It was a glorious day, and I could see the daffodils bathed in sunshine in the garden, a passing pheasant and, appropriately, a few Easter bunnies hopping around the lawn behind David with his clasped hands. Martin commented on the missing button on his sleeve, apparently as a result of the number of times people "pass" upstairs at home and have to be carried downstairs on their final journey by David, who presumably brushes against the wall or the banisters. I was glad our Little Lady went the way she did as a result, and her little coffin wouldn't have been wide enough to brush against anything on either side.

We wanted daffodils, and a small hand bouquet of snowdrops for her funeral – I wasn't quite sure how we would carry the snowdrops but knew how important they were symbolically. Martin had already decided to carry her coffin into the crematorium with me beside him – not that she's heavy, but I'm not supposed to carry anything still and I'm not sure I could manage it anyway.

We chose a humanist to carry out the service, which David is arranging. We agreed not have a hearse as I think it would kill me to drive behind a car with such a tiny coffin lost in the middle of it, so we'll meet her at the crematorium instead. It seems odd arranging cars to leave the house, as it was less than a year ago that Martin and I were arranging our wedding car to take us up to Stirling Castle. It was a 1926 classic Rolls Royce–it reminded me of Thomas the Tank Engine as it was an identical colour of blue. The cars on Wednesday will be black – 7 adults split between 2, so we'll be able to travel there on our own, with the rest of the family in the car behind us. One of the options was to have her in the car with us, but we've already said our Goodbyes here at home.

David took her with him, so we'll see her for our final farewell on Wednesday......................

Although we decided not to use it, as neither of us are religious, David left a beautiful verse that we felt mirrored sentiments that would have been appropriate if we had believed:

The Gift

I'll lend you a child for a little while,
"a child of mine" god said
For you to love the while she lives, and mourn
for when she's dead.
It may be six or seven years, or forty two or three.
But will you till I call her back, take care of her for me?
She'll bring her charms to gladden you,
and should her stay be brief,
You'll always have her memories as a solace for your grief.
I cannot promise she will stay since all from Earth return,
But there are lessons taught below
I want this child to learn.
I've looked the whole World over, in search of teachers true,
And from the things that crowd life's way,
I have chosen you.
Now will you give her all your love,
nor think the labour vain?
Nor hate me when I come to take
this lent child back again?
I fancied that I heard them say
"Dear Lord thy will be done",
For all the joys thy child will bring,
the risk of grief we'll run.
We'll shelter her with tenderness,
we'll love her while we may,
And for the happiness we've known, forever grateful stay.
But should thine Angels call for her
much sooner than we'd planned,
We'll brave the bitter grief that comes,
and try to understand.

Amen

"What Was She Like?"

We could only cope with one major task each day, so had decided to see the humanist at 12 o'clock on Monday. Mary Wallace had done Saz's sister Lisa's wedding to Michael at Stirling Castle the previous August, so was a perfect choice by David. I later found out that Lisa had also called her to see whether she had been approached to do Amélie's service that Wednesday. The flowers from Lisa and Michael were the flowers we'd chosen for our own wedding – a thoughtful touch.

Mary spent an hour and a half with us, getting to know us as a couple, and wanting to find out as much as she could about my pregnancy, the rollercoaster we'd been through away from home on the Wirral, and about Amélie. She had lost two babies, so genuinely understood our grief. We were having a bad day that day, and knew that there'd be many more like that to come, but Mary's empathy was an invaluable support to me – one mother to another. Martin could barely speak as I relived our experience with Mary. She encouraged me and made me believe that not only was none of it our fault, but that everything we were doing was a good positive thing to do – writing this book, talking about Amélie, planting her Garden, raising money for the SCBU (Wirral Hospital Trust Fund 939 for any donations please).

An incredibly compassionate, genuine and caring woman, who even put snowdrops on the funeral service she created and read from:

A celebration of the life of

Amélie Charlotte Tewkesbury

6th March 2005 – 17th March 2005

Falkirk Crematorium, 23rd March 2005

Composed and conducted by
Mary Wallace, Registered
Officiant, Humanist Society of Scotland
(*Music: Robbie Williams, 'Angels'*)

Good afternoon. We are here today to celebrate the little
life of Amélie Charlotte Tewkesbury, much loved daughter
of Sarah and Martin. I am Mary Wallace, from the
Humanist Society of Scotland and I have been asked to
conduct a simple humanist funeral for Amélie today.
Although today's ceremony will be non-religious,
there will be time later on for quiet reflection
and private prayer.
I know that it was important for Sarah and Martin
to share this ceremony with the people who are really
important in their lives – and that is you, their family
and close friends, the special people who have been there
for them when they needed them most. And they have
also asked me to say that not only have they lost their
precious daughter, but their parents, John and Liz and
Sylvia have also lost a granddaughter. Duncan, Sarah,
Rob and Nicky have lost a niece, and friends and
other family have lost a little girl they'll never have the
privilege of knowing.

This is a sad day and I know that you will all still be struggling to come to terms with your loss. It is impossible not to reflect on the fact that Amélie's death is untimely and unfair. Those who have lived long and well – and those close to them – can often face death with a calm acceptance of what is part of the natural order of things. We may grieve, but we can more readily accept that their life has been lived and has drawn to an inevitable close. But the death of a wee one is so much harder to bear. We not only mourn the life that was, but also the life that might have been. It seems a cruel breach of an unwritten law to lose a baby like Amélie, whose life had only just started. At times like this, you might ask 'why us?' and 'why Amélie?'. But there are no answers and sadly, there probably never will be.

It is hard to find any words of comfort at a time like this – when words say so little and tears so much. It will sometimes feel as if the grief you carry in your hearts is too much to bear. But if you let it run its course, it will, like a river, eventually empty into a calmer sea of acceptance. The tears of despair will, in time, turn to tears of a different kind – tears of sorrow, but of a peaceful sorrow, a gentle kind of sadness, a centred kind of grief. Sorrow of course also goes hand in hand with love and the depth of your sadness is a reflection of how much you loved little Amélie.

Despite our sorrow today, Sarah and Martin wanted this ceremony to be a celebration of Amélie's life. So I hope that you will feel able not just to cry for her today, but also to smile as you focus on the love and joy she brought into your lives during her brief stay.

As the card from their friends Srirat and David said:

"A size so small...
A love so big...
A girl so special....."

"Each precious new baby arrives with unique gifts and needs, but one thing they all share is the amazing ability to give and receive love."

It is important to hold onto the fact that when Amélie died she was very much loved. She was at the centre of Martin and Sarah's world for the 11 days of her life. She knew her Mum and Dad and responded to them and the precious moments they spent with her can never ever be taken away. She also gave them the gift of being able to say goodbye to her, to be able to hold and cuddle her..... Her time had come, but in her own sweet little way, she made the letting go easier for her Mum and Dad.

Although in one sense, you will feel that you have lost her, in many other ways, Amélie is still and always will be a part of your lives. The time you shared with her was short, but it was also precious and lasting.

It had been a wonderful pregnancy and Martin and Sarah could not have been more delighted with the news of their honeymoon baby. They were delighted too when they found out that she was a girl and the bond was already strong even before she was born. They chose her name because they have an affinity with France and particularly love the film 'Amélie'. For those of you who don't know it, the film is different, unique and quirky. It is also impossible not to make comparisons – the film is a story about a lovely innocent young girl who helps to make other people's lives happier with little acts of kindness and love. I'm sure you'll agree that despite what has happened, those words could apply to our little Amélie too. Her middle name is Charlotte and Sarah and Martin chose this as a special way to remember Martin's Dad, Paul whose first name was actually Charles and who sadly died in December. But I gather that he was delighted to know that they were expecting a wee girl – as indeed the rest of the family were too.

When Amélie was born unexpectedly early three Sundays ago, she was very poorly, but she was also perfect and one of the Neo-Natal Nurses put this traditional little verse onto the side of her incubator:

> *"Monday's child is fair of face*
> *Tuesday's child is full of grace*
> *Wednesday's child is full of woe*
> *Thursday's child has far to go*
> *Friday's child is loving and giving*
> *Saturday's child works hard for a living*
> *But the child that's born on the Sabbath day*
> *Is good and kind, sweet and gay"*

Even when it became sadly obvious that Amélie was not going to make it, she still fought on, giving Sarah and Martin many beautiful and unforgettable moments with their precious daughter. I'd like to read a letter that Sarah wrote to Amélie last Tuesday. Sarah and Martin have asked me to share this with you because it encompasses their feelings:

15th March 2005

Dearest Amélie

As I sit here by your incubator, I feel very proud to be your Mummy, and Daddy and I are privileged to have you as our precious daughter. No-one knows why you're so ill and James told us yesterday that you wouldn't cope without the machines you're on at the moment.

So Daddy and I have decided to spend as much time as we can with you, cuddling you and memorising every millimetre of your perfect little body. You've got Daddy's ears, big feet and long legs, his dimpled chin, my slim waist and long back and the most beautiful deep midnight blue eyes imaginable.

We've had a rollercoaster of emotions since you were born last Sunday, March 6th, weighing 2.36 kg. But the most overwhelming emotion throughout has been absolute, unconditional, overpowering love – if there were anything Daddy and I could do to make you better and keep you with us, we'd do it without hesitation.

You've touched many people during your time here at Arrowe Park – all the consultants and nurses have said what a perfect, beautiful girl you are. And you can't begin to imagine how much you are loved by the rest of the family who've met you – Nonna and JB, Nanna, Duncan, Sarah and Rob. They've bought you some lovely little dresses that you look incredibly gorgeous in and some Easter bunnies to watch over you while we try to sleep upstairs in the Snowdrop Room. We're going to plant snowdrops to make an Amélie garden at Chartershall, Horseshoes, Chiswick and Wimbledon and will make a huge photo album of all the photos we've taken of you. You're absolutely unique and irreplaceable and will always be loved, remembered and adored by us all. One day we'll tell your siblings all about our special beautiful little lady that we've had the privilege of knowing.

It will be very difficult to say Goodbye when we have to, but you'll always be there in our hearts and minds.

Sleep well little lady.

We'll always love and treasure you,

Mummy and Daddy xxxxxxxxxxxxxxxxx

Try to remember that there are, even in the short time she was here, many lovely memories of Amélie to hold onto. Memories of the sweet and unmistakable sounds and smells of a new born baby. The memories of her lying contented and at peace in your arms.... These things you will never, ever forget. They are memories that you will carry with you always – with sadness, but also, in time, with a sense of peace in your hearts.

Before we say a formal farewell to Amélie, I'd like to read a final poem for you, chosen by Martin and Sarah for today:

"Mother of life,

Mother of death,
here is a spirit so new
that the gates of life and death
are just an archway in her dancing ground.
She has danced her way back to you.
Her passage is easy
But mine is hard.
I wanted to hold her living flesh
And feel her soft breath and her heartbeat.
(I nurtured her in my body;
I would have fed her from my breast)
I would have cared for her
And watched her first steps
And listened for her voice.
No other child that may come to me
Will ever be what she would have been.
Nothing, nobody, will ever replace her.
Whatever healing I may find,
this loss will always be a part of me.
(Bless my womb, which has the power
to create life and death)
Bless my arms
that would have embraced her.
Bless my hands that would have lifted her.
Bless my heart that grieves"

(From 'The Pagan Book of Living and Dying', by Starhawk,
M.Macha Nightmare and the Reclaiming Collective)

We have now, sadly, reached the part of today's ceremony when we will say a final farewell to Amélie. Immediately after the committal we will be listening to a lovely piece of music and I hope that this period of quiet reflection will help each of you to remember her in your own individual way or to pray privately if you would like to. Would you please stand for the committal?

In sorrow, but also in love and affection, we have been remembering Amélie's little life. Now it is time for us to let her go, in quietness of spirit.

Every living being has a beginning and an end.
For each of us, there is a time to be born and a time to die.
Now, as we say goodbye to Amélie,
we commit her to our memories with love
and we commit her body to its final end,
to rejoin the great cycle of nature.

Please be seated.

(Music: Giovanni Battista Pergolesi, 'Stabat Mater, Quando Corpus Morietur and Amen')

Amélie is at peace now, safe from the pain and hurt that this world may have brought her. In her little life, it is clear that she brought many gifts of joy and happiness to all of you. She was a brief, but bright ray of sunshine in your lives. And although clouds may now obscure that sunshine, it is still there and always will be. As little Olly says, Amélie has gone to be with the stars now and they of course will always be twinkling away in the sky for you.

Amélie also leaves a legacy of love for all of us, touching our lives in many different ways and reminding us all of what is really important in life. If it is possible to take anything away from this tragedy, let it be this – love is what joins us to one another and it is the only really important thing in our lives. Amélie brought family and friends together and if it was possible, brought Sarah and Martin even closer as a couple. They have been incredibly positive and strong – as individuals, as a couple, as parents and as a family unit. They are an inspiration to all of us.........

On behalf of Sarah and Martin, could I thank you all for coming along today to share in this ceremony of farewell to Amélie. I know that your kindness and support has been very much appreciated. There are too many people to thank individually, but I know that you have each, in different ways, been there for Sarah and Martin and Amélie in the last few weeks. And I feel sure that all of you will continue to offer your love and support over the coming weeks and months too. And as you do, never be afraid of tears and never be afraid to speak of Amélie or to use her name. In that way, you will keep her memory alive and that in itself is perhaps the most important and positive thing that any of you can do.

There will also be a collection after the ceremony for the Neo-Natal Unit at Arrowe Park Hospital in Upton on the Wirral. I gather that the staff there were wonderful, treating Sarah and Martin and Amélie with great respect, dignity and tenderness. Everything that could possibly have been done for her was done. There were, I believe, even times when that unique Scouse sense of humour kept them going with some smiles and laughter! So, if any of you would like to make a contribution to this most worthwhile cause, to help other babies in the future, there will be a collection plate in the hallway as you leave. And please note everyone that Sarah is on a mission – to raise as much money as she can! So dig deep folks! And don't worry if you've only got a £20 note just now – you can always supplement it later with a cheque for £200 - payable by the way, to the 'Wirral Hospital Trust Fund 939'! Seriously, any contribution you can make would be very much appreciated and will make a real difference.

You are also most warmly invited back to the house just now and I hope that when you go back, you'll be able to share your memories and enjoy a toast to a very special little girl. I'm sure you'll all understand that Martin and Sarah don't feel able to do the formal line up and hand shaking here at the Crematorium, but they would be delighted to see you all back in the more relaxed and peaceful surroundings of the house.

As we leave just now, I hope that it will be with a sense of peace as you remember the joy and the happiness that little Amélie brought into your lives. May that sense of peace be with you always.

Thank you.

(Music: Eva Cassidy, 'Over The Rainbow')

I changed my mind about the formal line up and hand shaking and wanted to see our friends. Their pain had been obvious as we arrived to see their huddled little group waiting for us outside the Crematorium and I wanted the first outburst to be somewhere other than at home. Rat looked about half everyone else's height.

On the way to the Crematorium earlier, Martin and I had both felt strangely calm and certainly very glad that we were in a car on our own. Lawrence, the driver, ate boiled sweets all the way, and we passed the William Simpson Home where my Grandpa spent his final days on the way. I knew he and my father-in-law Paul would keep an eye on Amélie wherever they were – Martin laughed and said it was more likely she'd be keeping an eye on them.

On the way back, Lawrence drove at a normal speed as we headed for home – Martin and I in the very back, the daffodils and snowdrops in front, and the funeral collection and envelope from Mary Wallace in my hands. I've never been very patient, so opened Mary's envelope to find a beautiful card and copy of the service inside. She'd also given us a pink heart-shaped candle – Amélie looked good in pink, and I'd already vowed to wear it more often, in some desperate attempt to connect with our daughter for the rest of my life.

I ran upstairs as quickly as my internal bruising would allow when we arrived home, so that I met our friends in the jeans I'd worn when she died. They all commented on how good I looked, but I knew the inner scars would never heal, even if disguised externally.

I took them into the lounge, so they could see the photos we'd taken on St. Patrick's Day – I wanted everyone to know what our beautiful baby looked like, but only took my 3 remaining bridesmaids Pam, Saz and Browning to see the more private photos in my childhood bedroom of our little Amélie with all her tubes in. My fourth bridesmaid Coolie had of course both seen the photos and met our precious girl, her niece.

Pam, my Chief Bridesmaid, hadn't been with us in that very bedroom the last time we were all supposed to be there together on our wedding day, as my Goddaughter Kiera was due any day then. She and Amélie were supposed to grow up together. But I figured there would be reminders for me for the rest of my life, and if not, I would make connections even where none existed.

Once everyone had been given a glass of our wedding champagne, I dragged Olly away from the popup book he was reading, gave him his token little glass of bubbly and made a toast

"To Friends, Family and Amélie" and inevitably burst into tears.

I later wondered whether I should have said "Family" first, then realised that our families knew how much they meant to us.

Mum's response was "To Saz and Martin, her remarkable parents" and inevitably burst into tears.

We didn't then, and still don't feel remarkable. What's tragic is the number of infant deaths we have since been exposed to. At least I'd recovered sufficiently physically to be able to enjoy my daughter without being drugged up to the eyeballs (another ridiculous notion), and we'd had 11 very special unforgettable days with her. So many parents have to give birth to a dead baby, or cope with one who only survives a matter of hours or minutes. In my mind, they'll always be far worse off than us.

We all walked down to the bottom lawn and Amélie's Garden – her tree had already blossomed since being planted the day before, as had the snowdrops. Marge was pleased with the placing of her perfect present.

It was a perfect day. The sun was shining.

Good Friday Pilgrimage

Martin and I had decided to walk up the Crags on that final part of the journey alone. It's a traditional trek close to home that takes its travellers to the top of a set of small cliffs overlooking the mountains, reservoir, and peaceful countryside – a familiar and favourite scene not only to me, but to Martin too in the years we've been together.

Our usual tipple at the top is whisky from a hipflask, however our drink of choice to toast the Little Lady was Guiness, a mere 8 days after our painful St. Patrick's Day.

Martin planted the last bunch of snowdrops, fittingly taken from beside the bridge at home where Martin proposed, and the remaining bunch of crocuses from Saz, watched over by Amélie's Easter bunny Snowdrop.

We took our final photos, and I shot the last piece of video to end the treasured footage of our sad story – my commentary stopped as the sun went down. The resulting DVD is the only "live" coverage we have of our precious daughter and will be watched in times of joy and sorrow for years to come. A particularly poignant part of it is when Olly describes how he says "Night Night Amélie" who's now "in the stars 'cos she wasn't feeling very well". I'm pleased he and Rosie will be able to see what their little cousin looked like when they're old enough not to find the hospital footage too disturbing. She'll always be a key part of our family.

Hurdles and Milestones

I made a conscious decision the day after Amélie died to get out of bed as soon as I woke up each day, and have done ever since. The prospect of merely getting through each day is a challenge that often seems utterly futile, and my concern was, and still is, that if I stayed in bed I wouldn't actually get up all day. There's not much incentive when I should have been looking after our little girl and she's not there. And she never will be. So the tasks are much needed.

I'd already decided to get individual presents for all the staff who looked after our little Amélie so well at Arrowe Park, along with as much money as I could raise for the SCBU equipment itself.

Once the outcome with Amélie was inevitable and we were still staying in the Snowdrop Room, I wrote down the surnames of all the staff who had looked after us and whom we intended to buy a gift for – I'd been jotting down things during the long nights that might be appropriate for each of them – a DIY manual for James, lime midget gems and ski hand warmers for Pauline, an ice bucket for Lynne (she'd given us a medical syringe bucket for the champagne from Dunk we celebrated Amélie's life with the first Saturday after she was born), a book on Australia for Tracy, and so the list went on.

Dad had put Martin on his car insurance as I still wasn't allowed to drive for another 4 weeks, so we drove into Stirling and I desperately hoped we wouldn't meet anyone I knew, as usually happened on my present-buying sprees in my home town.

The Thistle Centre, as it always was during the day, was even more full of young Mums and ugly babies than usual, and three of the shop assistants who served us that day were pregnant. I soon realised that I would, unintentionally, find a connection with Amélie in every-thing I did, saw, said and was a part of for the foreseeable future and beyond.

I had lost it in the shop we bought the photo albums in and silently broke down, knowing we were choosing frames for the photos to share on her funeral day and to cherish for years to come. I was acutely aware that the colour scheme had to match our dining room at home in Chiswick, then remembered the birth ball that would still be in the sitting room, car seat in the hall, buggy in the kitchen, breast pump in the cupboard that I would have to face at some point before even tackling the walk upstairs to Amélie's perfectly prepared room. I vowed that Martin and I would clear her belongings ourselves and turn the room temporarily back into a room for Olly, Rosie, Kiera, Lieve, Max or Madeleine to stay in – I didn't want anyone else touching her things and wiping the memories as if she'd never been born.

I also needed more breast pads, and was very pleased when I managed the Boots maternity and baby section on my own without tearily hyperventilating. Martin joined me as I was in the queue for the till, and the woman in front had no control at all over the little girl roped by baby reins to her waist. I knew we would never have chosen or needed to tie Amélie to us and I felt bitter at her perceived ineptitude as a mother – it's increasingly easy to bring up other people's kids.

Virgin Megastore made me weep – somehow it seemed really sad that the copy of the Amadeus soundtrack we had bought for the one choral piece at her funeral was corrupt and their last copy. Nothing lasted any more.

And I noticed far more handicapped people than ever previously – maybe there were no more than usual, but I looked at them in a very different way after our experience with Amélie, and thought what a pointless exercise it would be for us in the future to check whether any baby I were carrying were Downs Syndrome – at least they're happy and healthy and genuinely enjoy life. And life rather than just living is a differently perceived concept to us both now.

I managed to phone Stem Cells International, the company we'd decided to use for stem cell storage from the umbilical cord should Amélie ever become ill. I broke down on having to tell them why we no longer needed the collection kit to be dropped off but that we hoped to use their services at some point in the future.

Equally difficult were the cold calls I received from baby clothing companies, children's bookstores or just companies cold calling for unrelated products – all got sharp responses to their questions, and having to say "Now isn't a good time. My daughter's just died." somehow made it more real and my old reality even further out of reach.

I still can't bring myself to phone the nursery where we'd reserved a place for Amélie on my return to work. Let's hope we will need their services at some point.

I treated myself to a massage after Martin had returned to London and I was on my own with my parents. The form asked for notification of any recent operations and I realised it was only 3 weeks since my Caesarean – major surgery and it was therefore the first time I had had to lie on my stomach since. I just said quietly "She didn't make it", knowing I would have to state that on many an occasion in the future – lying there I visualised my business card holder at work and the number of people that would have to be told. At my next massage I didn't manage to be quite so brave, and sobbed when the beautician said "Wow, for someone who had a C-section so recently you look fantastic!" She wasn't to know.

One day it must become easier.

Guiness and Chips

The day after Amélie's funeral, Mum had organised a doctor's appointment for me, to ensure I had a medical professional checking my physical state and healing progress. The doctor I saw was a lovely woman, who of course made me cry by asking the simple question "What can I do for you today?". Explaining our situation to strangers will always be more difficult, as I have less of a problem breaking down with friends and those dear to me.

She checked and confirmed I was in good shape physically and my body recovering speedily from the Caesarean. I'd been taking arnica to aid the internal and external bruising, which appeared to have helped, although my stomach around the scar itself was still very numb and tingly and I'm sure will be for some time. Time then to check my mental wellbeing and discuss ongoing recovery.

My placenta had been sent to the pathology lab for testing, although I was convinced that any results would not be able to shed light on the cause of Amélie's sudden problem in the womb. My blood tests immediately after delivery were completely normal, as were Amélie's, so we were both a bit of an anomaly to the medical profession – "Just one of those horrific freaks of nature" was the only explanation ever given to me, which we'll just have to accept and live with. But I was keen to ensure that any problem was not likely to be genetic, so quizzed this poor doctor about trying for another baby and how I could give myself the best chance physically of returning to my fit and healthy state. Amélie will always be absolutely irreplaceable, but we were both desperate to pour our love into another mini Tewkesbury.

The doctor's response amused me. "Light exercise like swimming, walking and light weights" – she had clearly never done any weight lifting in her life, and I estimate her to have weighed around 18 stone. If she had, she would have realised that any type of weightlifting requires the use of one's "core" ie. stomach muscles!

In some ways, there is great satisfaction to be gained in my new routine of swimming and walking on a daily basis, and therefore slowly returning to my previous slim physique (I hope). But it comes with a feeling of great sadness, as the closer I become to returning to my former size and shape, the less I look like I ever gave birth – it feels like that sometimes.

After my emotional outburst at the doctor's, I felt like I needed cheering up, so Martin and I had a pint of Guiness in a local pub. It seemed strange to be surrounded by people laughing and joking sharing the grievances of their various days at work, as our lives had been turned so cruelly upside down. It was a mere 24 hours after our daughter's funeral, and the start of my fanatical clock- or calendar-watching. Sadly, I knew I would be able to find a marker each day, week or month for the rest of our lives. In the back of my mind, I anticipated with dread each of the 3 due dates we'd been given for Amélie, my eventual return to work (as I left there happily pregnant for a week's holiday), our wedding anniversary (as Amélie was conceived shortly afterwards), our next year's skiing holiday to Avoriaz (for obvious reasons), meeting Saz's daughter Summer for the first time (she was born a month before Amélie and would be a lifelong reminder for me) etc. etc. etc. Everywhere I looked there would be reminders, and if there weren't, on my worse days, I'd create them.

Sitting in the pub, we talked, held hands, I cried again, and suddenly decided I wanted to eat proper chip shop chips outside in the spring sunshine.

Paulino's on the Glasgow Road in Stirling does the best fish and chips I've ever eaten, and it was with wry amusement and a degree of sadness that I realised the woman serving me was the same woman who had served me during my schooldays on the rare occasions we were

ever allowed to eat chips. "Sal' en vinegar weethat hen?" –
I thought back to the Scouse accent and how used to it I'd
become.

We sat on the bench outside the house to eat our chips
and have another Guiness. It was freezing cold but there
was a beautiful sunset.

Sympathy Sucks

Nobody knows what to say.

Nobody knows what to do.

We appreciate that, but there are two dreadfully
inappropriate extremes.

One old neighbour of ours came round to see us about
three weeks after Amélie died. I'll spare him the
embarrassment by not referring to him by name, but he
had written the most lovely email to Mum a fortnight
previously:

" Your email was forwarded to me. We are sincerely
sorry to hear your sad news. We both understand the
feeling of loss for all the family and send our love to Sarah,
Martin and of course everyone whose lives have been
touched by little Amélie Charlotte.

I hope to be in Stirling in the not too distant future and
perhaps, if suitable I could pop in for a few minutes to see
yourself and John.
Love to you all and please pass on our thoughts to Sarah."

When he arrived at our house, where I was still at home
with my parents recuperating, his opening question to us
all was a cheery "So how are we enjoying life then?". I
thought I'd give him the benefit of the doubt and assume
that he was made to feel uncomfortable by the fact I was
there and he really didn't know what to say, so didn't

really comment or, at that stage, pass judgement. However, after an hour and a half of hearing about his latest achievements, trials and tribulations without so much as a "How are you?" to any of us, I was absolutely gobsmacked. My 3 year old nephew showed more empathy than this 57-year old man who had known me for 24 years..... After he left, I actually laughed out loud at his complete inadequacy and wondered whether he'd somehow forgotten the tragedy that had so recently devastated our family. I guess I'll never know.

The other extreme usually involves the head to one side, sometimes outstretched arms and a very sympathetic expression. I can't deal with it. I can't deal with people being too nice, as their overly compassionate looks are like a huge trowel digging up the pain, which is never very far from the surface.

Everyone grieves in different ways and at a different pace. I've discovered this through being with my nuclear family and Martin's until just after Amélie's funeral. For all of us though, it's a slow and painful process.

I've found it immensely helpful to set my sights on mini achievements – writing this book ; swimming every day to return to my previous fitness level; writing to all the generous souls who have contributed to my fundraising mission; making copies of the DVD for our family with my own personalised covers; walking in the fresh chilly Scottish air; making a few token phone calls when I think I can cope with the harsh reality of hearing myself say out loud "She died in our arms, where she belonged." I do genuinely feel privileged to have spent the 11 very special days we had with our precious daughter, but miss her desperately and ache at the thought I'll never be able to hold her again.

Dad's the only other person who could bring himself to watch the DVD, so he and I have a shared experience that we talk about when we're alone – sometimes fondly, sometimes in excruciating pain. Mum has only just managed to write the first letter and has been procrastinating about it for days. I don't really know about my beloved Martin, as I haven't seen him for 3 weeks now while he's been back in London and at work. I'm very much looking forward to us being together again and being on our own to start grieving, which we haven't had the chance to do since any of this happened.

Technology too has its downfalls. By downloading some of the beautiful photos of Amélie to copy onto my DVD covers, as they are such large file sizes I am often confronted with a message on the screen saying "Amélie – not responding". This sad truth will undoubtedly confront me on my first dreaded day back at work, whenever I feel ready to face that hurdle.

I cry a lot – sometimes a silent stream of tears down my cheeks, sometimes sobbing aloud in the way small children do – downturned mouth, gulping for the air my daughter never inhaled properly. The frightening thing is that it doesn't necessarily take anything specific to set me off – I'm suddenly overcome with an overwhelming sense of grief and need to alienate those around me – sometimes, on the other hand, I need to be held. There are no rules, which is difficult.

But Why?

We'll never know what went wrong to cause our precious Amélie's lack of oxygen on that fateful Sunday and her subsequent coma and breathing problems. Sometimes I do feel bitter and that it's all grossly unfair; at other times I feel privileged to have enjoyed the time we were lucky enough to have with her. One thing I cannot feel is that it was "for a reason", or that "it wasn't meant to be" or was "nature's way" when all had been perfectly normal a mere 24 hours before Amélie had to be delivered in such an unexplicable emergency.

In my more philosophical moments, I can feel that in some way it was better that I didn't go to hospital sufficiently early that day to mean that Amélie ended up alive but not properly living with any real quality – she may not have been able to eat, speak or walk unaided and at least she was never in any pain or discomfort and kept her dignity.

I do sometimes wonder how those who, unlike us, believe in God, can possibly justify such pain and suffering, especially as victims who have never inflicted pain on others. Sylvia, Amélie's Nanna, encompassed those feelings of struggling with her faith perfectly in a poem she wrote on returning from her trip to Scotland for Amélie's funeral:

How Dare You!

I was called to your side to meet you. I got to know you and love you so much in our brief time together.
As I travel on the train the students laughed and planned their lives.

How dare you!

When I get to that place where your brief life was held in grace, your mother, father, uncles, aunts and your grand-parents watching your every struggle, the noise and the bustle. The doctors, the nurses and other parents eat and laugh and show their babies.

How dare you!

As we watched your struggles and dressed you in the pretty clothes, new parents out of mind and head gave birth to children long neglected;
They thrived and grew strong and watched us with smiling eyes.

How dare you!

We shopped for your Mummy and Daddy and bought you dresses and toys.
We walked around the shops and people got on with their lives.
People planned what would happen if you lived or died.

How dare you!

When I got home so many of your family rang to wish you and your Mummy and Daddy well. I tried to close my ears to their love and concern.
I didn't know how to speak of you and your Grandad leaving us.
How could they know I had prayed and prayed.

How dare you!

As I travel back to Mummy's home to see you join your Grandad, all the happy families around me happily speak of the Easter holiday.
The traditional time of new life, the spring flowers bursting and the birds and animals thriving with new life.

How dare you!

We stand and listen to the humanist give hope.
Friends and family watch your tiny casket enter into

eternal life.
We stand outside greeting and hugging each other
And speak of comfort I cannot join in

How dare you!

We go back to the house they eat, they drink and laugh
and give us hope.
You took it all away.

How dare you!

You give life and hope, took this beloved child so wanted.
So loved, so cherished
You decided she was too good to stay with us.

Dear God How Dare You.

Madness on Mull

Martin and I decided to have a break away from all things familiar so, as I was unable to fly, opted for a tour of the west coast of Scotland. We'd originally planned to do this trip with Saskia and Taco, and will undoubtedly share it with them at some point in the future, but for now being on our own was the most important thing imaginable. We desperately needed to talk about Amélie, cry together and relax away from anyone we knew.

We spent a night in Inverary our first night away and I drank so much red wine I was very poorly the following day and had to get Martin to stop the car so I could be sick. He laughed at my pathetic hungover state, but I got my revenge later in the week after a particularly heavy drinking sessions with our new friends Katie and Laurence – more to follow on that front.

Night number two was spent in a fabulous place that I'd eaten at previously with the rest of the Speake crew, the Pierhouse at Port Appin, who serve the most superb seafood. It's difficult though, never knowing when the tightening throat is going to consume me and restart the flow of tears that is never very far from the surface, and that evening I wept into my salmon fishcakes – Amélie should have been on the floor beside me in her car seat while we ate; the family picture I'd envisaged in my head so very often during my pregnancy. It seemed so unfeasibly sad going to bed that all we had with us instead were Amélie's portrait in the beautiful frame my friend Al had given me and the blanket that she was wrapped in when she died.

The next morning we walked along the beach and decided to head further north through Fort William. It was torrential rain in Fort William, so we headed for the Mull ferry, aiming for the south side of the island. I phoned Mum to check exactly where Tiroran House was, an excellent family home that did bed and breakfast that our friends Lisa and Michael had spotted online but never stayed in. All the other places I'd found were too far north, and Tiroran House turned out to be on the south side, on the north bank of Loch Scridain. We didn't bother checking beforehand whether they had space for that night, so turned up on spec and fate led us to a haven we will return to many times in the future.

I got excited as we drove up the drive through the rhodedendrons as it reminded me of my childhood home. Laurence met us at the door and asked whether we were the Thompsons, who presumably had booked in advance. While he went off to check with "Senior management" (Katie) whether they had space for us that night, we soaked up the atmosphere – the welcoming smell of freshly baked bread, the roaring fire in the sitting room overlooking the loch and the overwhelming feeling that we'd fortuitously ended up in a very relaxing, elegant home from home. I literally skipped around our enormous room after Laurence had closed the door behind him, immediately feeling at peace having been recommended that we "chill out and read the papers while we bring you some tea and homemade scones" – it was only then we realised we hadn't eaten all day.

So chill out we did! We arrived at Tiroran on the Sunday night and eventually left mid afternoon on the Thursday, having initially intended to stay one night only. Monday's weather was diabolical, but as we'd decided to go for a 14 mile walk to the Fossil Tree, off we went in the pouring rain. I howled for the first few miles, feeling so utterly empty and desolate, wishing I could somehow turn back the clock and make it all better as I clutched Martin's hand. At least we were back together and had finally had the chance to talk and cry (a lot) for our precious daughter. I felt an enormous sense of achievement at what turned out to be a treacherous and challenging cliff walk so soon after my all-clear from the doctor, which somehow reaffirmed my belief that I could cope with difficult things again. The other guests had left by the time we returned to Tiroran, and as we walked around the headland where the house came into sight, we looked forward to stripping off our soaking, muddy clothes and bathing in the massive bath in our en-suite. I was still so tired after eating yet another of Katie's fabulous meals that evening that I took myself off to bed and left Martin downstairs by the fire.

The next morning when I woke up, Martin's first words were "I've got some news for you". It transpired that he'd spent a fair amount of time with Laurence and Katie and a bottle of port the previous evening after I'd gone to bed. Katie had spotted Amélie's photo by my bedside and the book I was reading about how to survive the death of one's baby and inevitably had put two and two together correctly. They'd realised the importance to us of having a haven away from the rest of the world, so had suggested to Martin we stay at Tiroran that night (Tuesday) and housesit for them while they took Laurence's kids back to school in Edinburgh. It was the second time I'd skipped around the room and we jumped at the chance to look after the house, dog and cat for these people we had barely known 2 days previously, yet who had quickly become our saviours and very, very dear friends. For that to happen at any stage in people's lives is special, but for us all the more special as it happened at a time when we seriously needed to be with lovely people – an added bonus that it was in such spectacular surroundings. By our account and theirs, many would say it was utter madness for them to leave their house and livelihood in the hands of two almost strangers in terms of how long we'd know each other, but it just felt right.

Tiroran proved a perfect base from which to visit Fingals Cave on Staffa, walk along the spectacular cliff paths, explore Mull, hop over to Iona or just chill out and enjoy the peace and tranquility. I lit a candle for Amélie in Iona Abbey the day we got the short ferry over to the island, and it was the first time I'd managed to do something very symbolic in her memory without falling apart. The whole trip gave us both time to reflect on what may have been, what actually happened and the gaping hole in our lives we'd ended up with but were somehow beginning to accommodate as a fact that will never leave us, as indeed our treasured memories of Amélie never will.

Tiroran House and Katie and Laurence will be part of our lives forever though, and proved a shining light in the Scottish rain that fateful Sunday.

Home Bitter Home

I'd told Martin I'd be home around 7pm, as I knew he was keen to be there when I finally arrived back at our home in Chiswick, but I intentionally arrived home a couple of hours earlier to tackle it on my own. Martin had already faced the challenge of walking back into our home on his own, and I felt it only appropriate I also face the music alone. I knew Martin had already removed the car seat from the hall and Amélie's buggy from the kitchen, but her room was exactly as I'd left it 7 weeks previously – on Mothers' Day.

The house smelt slightly musty after noone really living in it and I stood in the doorway clutching the bag that held Amélie's ashes and keepsakes. I'd already decided where to put her, but walked round the house going into every room and breathing in the life I'd so reluctantly now irretrievably left for good. The house felt bigger than I remembered it, and as I looked out into the garden I thought about Martin's plans to turf it so that Amélie and I could spend as much of the summer and my maternity leave out in the garden as possible. I was getting used to facing shattered dreams – the harsh reality of having planned and imagined so much in my head.......... weekend barbeques with friends, with Amélie asleep in the shade ; walking round Kew Gardens with her in the 3-wheeler buggy we'd chosen so carefully; going into Soho to meet friends and colleagues for lunch with Amélie in her Baby Bjorn; driving to places with her fast asleep in her car seat; showing her off to friends and family; interrupted sleep where we'd be woken by her hungry cries............ none of these would be a reality now.

I left her room to last. As with most things, the reality was less bad than the anticipation ....her cot, changing mat, wardrobe full of little clothes on hangers with the price tags still attached, moses basket, blankets. I pictured her in the cot we could see through the door across the landing from our bedroom and the silent tears fell again. I knew we had to clear her things and put the kids' bed back in there, but wasn't ready to deal with it – maybe we'd manage it at the weekend. I certainly wasn't prepared to keep everything as it was and just shut the door as someone had unhelpfully suggested – shutting the door would never take away the memories and we desperately wanted to keep hold of the memories rather than try and erase them. When you've lost a baby and are grieving, sometimes it feels like everyone wants a piece of you – noone really knows how to react, what to say, what to do, but they all need to feel like they're helping and it's highly pressurising.

I put her urn on our dressing table and vowed that any time we went away, she'd have to come with us. Her ashes, keepsakes and the memories were the only things we had left, and my worst fear was that someone broke into our house, mistook her urn for a jewellery box and desecrated what little we had left of her precious body. I unpacked the photos from Arrowe Park and they, with her 3 Easter bunnies, form a pseudo shrine in our bedroom, where she should have slept in her first weeks in her moses basket. The rest of the photo frames are on the mantelpiece so that she's with us in the rooms we spend the most time in. The rest of the unpacking could wait.

I decided to go and see Paul & Hazel before Martin got back, so rang the doorbell of our neighbours two doors down in the knowledge that Paul would be at home working. He gave me a massive hug and cried when he saw me – I guess, as with so many others, imagining the pain of losing his own children, and seeing the pain contorting my face as on so many occasions in recent weeks. It was upsetting telling Paul & Hazel our sad little story, but important for them to know what happened so they could try and say the right things. It's always difficult when I see people again for the first time, and exhausting having to relive the tragedy time and again. Three glasses of wine and another hurdle down, I went home to wait for Martin.

We had a quiet evening and Martin approved of what I'd done with the photos and Amélie's ashes. This was our new life now – ashes, photos, a bag of keepsakes. And for me, the physical scare as a permanent reminder of the unexpected way our precious daughter came into the world.

The next day I needed to get birthday cards for Dad and Madeleine for the following week. As always, Chiswick High Road was full of the "yummy Mummy" brigade wheeling their bundles of joy around – that should have been me.

I went to see Pam and Kiera that afternoon, and showed Pam the photo album of our little lady. She cried when she saw the reality of our life in hospital as I knew anyone would who shared our sorrow. To cheer myself up, I went off to pick Olly and Rosie up from nursery. Olly skipped towards me in delight and Rosie walked towards me holding one of the care assistant's hands, grinning away. Pretty impressive at only 10 months old. I wondered if Amélie would have had a similar grin, or been so advanced in her achievements (of that I felt sure).

Courage then temporarily escaped me. I couldn't get out of the bed at all the following day – I woke up after Martin had left to play golf and looked at the dressing table. I felt so empty, broken and hollow. I was inconsolable, knowing that the support network would be monitoring me from afar – lovely text messages from Pam just pushed me further into the depths of despair now so familiar, yet I desperately didn't want to appear to be pushing her away. For the first time since Amélie's death, Martin couldn't help either. I didn't want to eat, sleep, breathe or be, and I so wanted to feel better as I knew he was hurting just as badly. I didn't have the energy to be supportive to anyone else that day.

The sun was shining that first weekend, so I sat in the garden watching Martin weeding the flowerbeds in my misery. Our neighbour Becky came out into her garden and said over the fence "It's good to see you back. I know you've got lots of friends, but I'm only next door, and if there's anything I can do, then let me know. It's good to see you back." Tears poured down my face and I nodded a silent "Thank you", incapable of speech. I knew I had so very many difficult conversations ahead - while everyone else's lives had continued as normal, ours had been cruelly halted, and even having the most basic conversations some days was phenomenally difficult.

Sally, our neighbour on the other side, also appeared in her garden later that day and we had a long conversation. As with so many people who know our sad story, they have a story of their own - one of Sally's publishing directors at work had given birth to a stillborn baby at 8 months' pregnant. I thought that would actually be worse than the situation we had been in – at least we had known and cuddled Amélie, proudly watched her respond to our touch, and seen her little face change in the last 3 days of her life while she was being fed my milk. Sally too said if we needed anything, even in the middle of the night, just to bang on the door. People have been so kind in their words and gestures, but there's nothing anyone can do to help:

Cold, detached, unfeeling
The care in me has gone
A shadow of the former me
My self does not belong

A part of me is missing
It's killed who I once was
My energy has gone on strike
I function just because

The hope for me is shattered
The dreams a shallow ghost
I do not wish to live now
Without my treasured most

Oh Amélie I miss you
My brain is always ticking
In sleep I feel happiest
Reality your kicking

The End Is Nigh

About six weeks after Amélie's death, I had to be in court in Edinburgh to defend myself for not paying for the pipe band that was supposed to, and didn't, play at our wedding. I drove up to Scotland on my own, relishing the time alone while I listened to CD after CD. I stopped for a quick break on the way and unintentionally ended up at Knutsford Services, where I'd stopped with the Arthurs on Mothers' Day. I felt achingly sad listening to Robbie Williams' "Angels", remembering how I'd felt on hearing it as we were ready to walk into the crematorium carrying Amélie's little coffin for her funeral. Eva Cassidy's *"Over the Rainbow"* forced the familiarly frequent stream of tears down my cheeks. I stopped wearing makeup weeks ago to prevent the telltale streaks down my face.

The agency that I'd booked the pipe band through lied in court, and I therefore spent a wasted day in very stressful surroundings only to lose the case. It was the last straw – I'd lost yet another thing in my life and it pushed me over the edge. When it became obvious I would be forced to pay the £600 AND this unprofessional agency's travel expenses, I burst into tears. It all seemed so futile and I couldn't wait to escape the thespian standing and sitting regime for a man in a ridiculous wig, against whose judgement I simply no longer had the energy to fight.

I wept all the way home, missing Amélie, missing the family life we'd no longer be able to enjoy with her, missing my old life where such pain didn't exist. The train rattled past the crematorium where we had had Amélie's funeral and I howled silently, wishing I'd brought my sunglasses to hide the questioning faces of my fellow passengers, who probably imagined me to be lamenting a lost love affair or something equally trivial in comparison to my harsh reality. I felt like screaming for them to stop looking at me with the imploring need of strangers to know the vile truth. Mum simply put her arm through mine when she met me at the station and didn't say a word. She didn't need to, and I knew my closest friends would hit me with a barrage of concerned text messages, asking how the case had gone. I really didn't have the energy to respond in detail, and hated the fact that I was being so closely monitored for signs of depression and gloom. I didn't want to be a member of the bereaved mothers' club, I didn't want to exert any energy on any of the relationships previously so important to me. I didn't see the point of life anymore.

We got home and I sat in the garden by the pond watching the fish, sobbing manically as I contemplated the most efficient ways of suicide. Shooting was too difficult as the only gun I had access to was Dad's air rifle, Scottish water was too cold to consider drowning, I'd inevitably throw up if I tried to overdose on pills………….. all in all, in the same way I couldn't carry Amélie successfully, and I'd failed to win a court case that prior to arriving at court was so clear cut, I knew I'd screw up suicide too, which exacerbated my absolute frustration. I recalled conversations about how selfish the act of suicide is for those that are left behind, but I was past that stage – failure of managing to kill myself successfully was the deterrent, not my relationship with Martin, family and friends and I realised I had hit an all-time low that I couldn't see ever changing. I screamed and shouted in despair at no particular audience and wished I was dead. At least then I wouldn't be without Amélie, and the pain I'd cause others by killing myself no longer mattered. Nothing mattered in this crap new life I was supposed to endure.

Mum realised the seriousness of my plight, and wept as she reminded me that I was as precious to her as Amélie was to me. I didn't care.

Nor did I care when I said I had NO hope left and Mum pointed out the hope for me and Martin in our relationship. I couldn't see that either. All I could see ahead was a life where the Sarah Speake playing at living was a translucent shadow of my former self – unsure, depressed and completely lacking in hope in any part of my life. I didn't want to be brave, I didn't want to hear that "time heals"(the wound of losing a child never heals, you just learn to live with it), I didn't want to speak to friends, I just didn't want to live without Amélie. I failed to see any glimmer of hope when Mum talked about Olly and Rosie. NOTHING and noone mattered and I wallowed in a mud of hate, sorrow and despair.

I had to drive to the airport to pick Martin up and Mum tried to persuade me not to drive – as I knew it would only go wrong if I tried to drive straight into a wall to end it all, I felt quite happy in reassuring her I'd be fine driving, and I needed to see Martin to check whether the numbness of feeling I was experiencing also extended to my feelings for him. He knew from the look on my face that I was "having a bad day" – my whole bloody life now is one "bad day" after the next and I just don't see the point in any of it. My former job seemed far too high profile and responsible to consider me ever being sufficiently recovered or in fact interested to return. The thought of Martin's birthday the following day and the inevitable charade while I tried not to ruin it for him by caring so little about life seemed a challenge I no longer cared to have the energy for either.

When I woke up on the morning of Martin's birthday, I realised that my recurrent dream of Amélie healthy and alive was just that – a dream that had become a nightmare by its unfair illusion. I went into Mum and Dad's bedroom to ask for sellotape to wrap Martin's presents and howled when Mum tried to get me to sit down on their bed and be hugged. It's the first time I my entire life I haven't bought and wrapped presents weeks in advance.

I tried to muster up the courage to seem fine while he opened his presents, painfully aware of Amélie's urn watching over us from the mantelpiece in my bedroom – she should have been lying in her moses basket gurgling at the first of her Daddy's birthdays she would witness and instead was a pile of dust in a box guarded by her Easter bunnies. I stood in the shower for far longer than normal that morning to hide away from the rest of the family, trying and failing to be cheerful. I had nothing to feel cheerful about. What was even the point of trying to get pregnant again as, knowing our luck, it would probably go wrong? I was painfully aware of the statistics on the SANDS website that 1 in every 100 babies born in England and Wales in 2003 were either stillborn or died in the first four weeks of their lives – why bother, as we would inevitably be one of those statistics. There was absolutely nothing to look forward to therefore, and I didn't see the point of planning anything in the future either as I felt so miserable. I didn't care that the sun was shining – it could have been snowing outside, and I would still have sat at the outside table with my head in my hands questioning the unfairness of it all. And for once, having Martin there didn't matter.

I was SO fed up of the pressure of well-meaning phone calls and text messages, encouraging me to continue in the futile quest for happiness, and annoyed that if I didn't respond people would worry. It's horrendous having to be monitored the entire time as people know you're unstable, and I no longer cared that anyone cared about me – a fat lot of good it did. I knew I was being selfish by avoiding the life jackets of support continually being thrown into my sea of unhappiness, but I wanted to sink. She was my baby, I was her mother, and I resented the grief being cosseted by others – how dare they wallow in something that wasn't rightfully theirs!

I have never felt so lonely.

> I don't want time to pass at all
> The weeks a constant marker
> Of more time lost since Amélie
> The strength of feeling darker
>
> Each Sunday now a day of pain
> Her birth an awful memory
> My life now lacking sun but rain
> Just pours unto eternity
>
> I've lost the will to live and smile
> Just being's not enough
> The cesspit that is now my home
> Reminds me that life's tough
>
> The hope I had has gone for good
> Our plans now dashed forever
> My biggest fear of time to pass
> Is that we might forget her

Rebuilding Our Lives

It's very difficult when the tasks run out.

For someone like me, who functions best with order and structure, usually that I've created myself, trying to get through each day without my usual level of routine was a phenomenal challenge. I've tackled difficult tasks before, whether workwise, in skiing down very steep mountains on or off-piste (I hate heights), doing the 73 mile Maggie's Monster Bike & Hike in May 2004, and so the list goes on.......

In some ways it was easier when we still had the funeral to organise, the video camera cartridge to be made into a DVD, the photos to develop and place in an album, the tree to plant, or even the money to raise.

But now there's nothing left to do except grieve.

And it's desperate.

I have good days and bad days, so the emotional roller-coaster continues. Everyone keeps telling me how strong and brave I am, but I feel very weak, unsure and panicky. Sometimes I can look at the photos of Amélie or the DVD and just feel immensely proud to be her Mummy, at other times my body convulses in sobbing pain that feels unbearable. I can see how people become alcoholics, in that the numbing from too much wine helps bring the day to an end, and to sleep without dreaming. The memories are too raw, and the sleep-induced hallucinations of Amélie as a healthy baby too painful to face.

I did manage to write to the nursery to let them know we no longer needed the place for Amélie while I was in Scotland early May, and the finality of it was somehow worse than the finality of taking her cot down the previous Monday. I also spoke with Sea France to alter our ferry booking for the end of May Bank Holiday and let them know that Amélie wouldn't be travelling with us (I had been reluctant to book a flight to France so early in her life as I thought flying at such a young age would be very bad for her little lungs – if only). I hadn't remembered how bookings are listed, and panicked when she said she had no record of an "Emily" travelling (people often get her name wrong when they hear it over the phone and, although it's like being skewered through the heart, I don't have the energy to correct them). She said "We do have a Miss A. Tewkesbury travelling. Is that the booking you'd like to cancel?" In my head I was screaming "No of course I don't want to cancel it. I don't want to cancel her life. I don't want to travel without her. I don't want to live without her." but I somehow managed to say calmly "Yes please" and she was merrily wiped from the booking and our trip to France.

I knew it would be difficult when we actually got to Dunk and Coolie's house in France. I'd been so looking forward to it, as it would be the first mini holiday my brother and I would have shared with our respective children. She should have been there with us. Thank God the distraction of Olly and Rosie would as always give me something to smile about.

Returning home to Chiswick after trips away is always difficult. After my trip home to Scotland for the court case and Martin's birthday, we took a detour to Donkley Wood in Northumberland to see the site where Amélie's trees (from Kate, Ade and Tom) and our wedding trees (from Lolo, Jeremy and kids) are planted. It's a beautiful part of the world, with so many newly-planted trees growing hope for the future and creating a haven for the local birdlife. Martin and I stood at the gate to the field thinking of Amélie, wrapped in our private thoughts, but both wondering how the hell we had ended up in this awful situation in the first place. I suppose for parents who choose to bury their children, there is some comfort in having a specific place (a cemetery) to visit to think about their lost baby or child. Although Donkley Wood gives us a non-religious equivalent, Amélie is with us in our hearts and thoughts continually and we think about her 24 hours a day, irrespective of whatever else we may be doing or saying at any given time. I asked Martin to save the location in our GPS system in the car, and silently pointed at the little red heart when he asked which symbol should be used to mark the spot.

I spoke very few words in the nine hour round trip home and simply stared into space, knowing that the following day would mark 2 months since Amélie's death and that once again I would dream of her living and wake up to the new life I so hated. Waiting for me at home in Chiswick was a letter from Annie, the Feeding Advisor I'd met in hospital and the woman responsible for the Wirral Milk Bank, that left me sobbing in despair – I felt unable to be excited or proud at the fact I had unknowingly already helped other sick or premature babies, both at Arrowe Park itself and a hospital in Manchester:

Dear Sarah & Martin,

Please accept my apologies for the delay in writing to you and hope this letter finds you both well.

I write to inform you Sarah that your blood screening tests were all clear and your milk was pasteurised on 30th March. Some has recently been despatched for babies at Arrowe Park. In addition, you might like to know that some has gone to St. Mary's hospital in Manchester (a busy regional neonatal medical and surgical NNU).

On behalf of those recipient babies & their grateful parents...... a big thank you. I hope it is some comfort to know that Amélie has helped in the recovery of other sick and premature babies.

Please accept the enclosed certificate of thanks for your kind donation of milk at a very difficult time.

Wishing you and your families the very best for the future.

Annie xxxx

The Wirral Mothers' Milk Bank

Certificate of Thanks presented to

Sarah Speake

who generously donated
1,400 mls
of her breast milk
at Wirral Hospital for the benefit
of sick and premature babies

signed AP. Atkinson   dated 9th May, 2005

As I suspected and partly dreaded, the 2 month anniversary of her death prompted calls from Saskia, Em, Saz, Pam, Rat, Coolie, Mum, Mhairi and Martin, all wishing beyond hope that they could persuade me my new life was worth living and trying not to pressurise me by prompting a response to monitor my state of mind after my suicidal wave the previous week that had so horrified them all. Marge (Saz's Mum) and Birgitte had also left messages on the answerphone that I simply couldn't conjure up the energy to respond to. I nobly agreed to have lunch and walk with Saz the following day and have dinner with Pammie and surprised myself by immediately feeling better that I'd actually managed to plan something in the future. But I still felt incredibly depressed, and my physical state wasn't helping. I so hankered to have the slim physique I had had to put no effort into maintaining before getting pregnant with Amélie, yet any more physical exertion than speedy walking made me bleed and meant I was still a stone heavier than at any time during my adult life and I didn't like myself for it. It simply added to my overwhelming depression.

Mum and Dad came down for the weekend during that period and, although I felt happy temporarily, and Olly and Rosie made me laugh and were a welcome distraction, I couldn't cope when we walked to the local park. Fat silent tears poured down my cheeks as I stood clutching Rosie's buggy in the middle of the children's playground, surrounding by the excited yelps of happy kids being watched over by proud parents. It was so unfair that we would never experience with Amélie such basic delights that so many parents take for granted. And, predictably as always, there was a young undeserving mother screaming at her kids, who were clearly so used to the torrent of irrational high-pitched yelling that they ignored her completely. I hated her.

That said, I do amaze myself sometimes, by genuinely feeling buoyant and seriously considering returning to work and normality. But for me I can never return to what was my normality. Life will never be the same again.

The Cloggie Has Landed

About eight weeks after Amélie died, Saskia called to say she would be in London the following week if I was up for a visit. I was absolutely delighted at the prospect of seeing my dear Dutch friend who had been so phenomenally supportive throughout our ordeal and continued to be. I also knew though, that it would be a highly emotional couple of days.

I'd spoken to Saskia's partner Taco a few weeks previously, and knew that he was finding it difficult to understand Saskia's devastation at our situation. Her emotional release would therefore be when she could allow herself the luxury of an outpouring of grief with me.

I picked her up from Heathrow and we hugged for ages. Inevitably, having held it together when I initially saw Sas, I lost it in the car on the way home. The sun was shining, so we spent the day outside talking about Amélie's birth, life and death and looking at the photos. Both of us needed to share the experience and shed many tears throughout the afternoon and evening, fuelled by about 2 bottles of wine each and, of course, the obligatory bottle of bubbly. Although I didn't realise it at the time or actually care about myself sufficiently to do something about it, my capacity for drinking copious amounts of alcohol was becoming the stuff of legends. It also meant that unfortunately, irrespective of how much I drank, I'd started dreaming about Amélie every single night without fail. And in my dreams she was healthy.

In one particularly disturbing recurrent dream, although I am conscious that Amélie has died, the faceless consultants tell me that they can put her back on the ventilator and breathe life back into her. I find it confusing even in my dream, as I can't understand how it would work when we've already had her funeral and I know her urn sits on our dressing table at home in Chiswick. But they do somehow manage to breathe life back into her and I hold and kiss her and can smell that unforgettable Amélie smell. And she opens her eyes to look lovingly into mine. I proudly present her to family and friends, who say "Oh Saz, she's absolutely beautiful." And then I wake up.

During her time with me, Sas asked me to be Lieve's Godmother. I felt very honoured to be asked, but saddened as I knew it had partially been fuelled by our situation with Amélie. It certainly formalised what was already an incredibly strong bond between us all and I looked forward to seeing my new Goddaughter on our summer holiday in France. I knew that Amélie's absence on that holiday would be acute, but then I'd become all too accustomed to continual disappointment, shock and pain.

On Saskia's last evening, we met up with another "cloggie" friend Annemiek, who had had twins the previous year who had also been in intensive care immediately after being born. I not only managed to hold it together with them both, I actually had a really good evening and thoroughly enjoyed myself. I felt like the old me, thriving on the buzz of being out in a bar with friends without feeling panicky about being out in public and surrounded by strangers. It was a breakthrough, in that I didn't feel guilty for feeling happy and having a good time either. Maybe I was slowly venturing on the road to recovery.

Tears and Tapestry

The day after Sas' visit, Martin and I set off for France. I was really excited at the prospect of having a mini holiday, and certainly looking forward to spending some time with Martin on our own before arriving at Dunk and Coolie's house a couple of days later. We had Amélie (we refer to her urn simply as "Amélie" as that's all we have left of her body) in the back of the car, and we both felt calmed by her presence. As the ferry left Dover with its white cliffs and I had Amélie in a rucksack at my feet, I wept. Wept at the loss, wept at us nearing France and the holiday that should have been her first trip abroad, wept at the sadness of having a rucksack with an urn rather than her in her carseat with us............... I felt sorry for Martin, who was also desolate in our loss and at a loss as to what to do to help my sad state. But as I'd mastered so well, I recovered relatively quickly and we started looking at our book of chambre d'hotes to plan how far we drove the first night and where we stayed en route to the house in Plessala.

We stopped at a town called Abbeville for a beer on the way and soaked up the atmosphere – baking sunshine in a little French market square, a cold beer and the prospect of a lovely break away from our new normality. The waitress was wonderfully rude and wonderfully French and we both felt happy. The converted manor house that we had booked into for the night was set in beautiful grounds and had a four poster bed, so we'd done it again – found a very special place to stay in a fabulous area. We drove into the local town of Eu and realised that not one single restaurant was open, so walked into the local boulangerie thinking we may well end up having to eat plain bread and cakes – oh the joys of being in France! We had no idea whether Wednesdays generally in this particular part of France were the local day off, but asked whether there were any restaurants in the local area that might be open. We were directed to the next town of Tréport and found a seafront and harbour with a superb row of excellent seafood restaurants.

After an amazing meal we returned to our temporary home for the night and I was hit with a wave of grief. It always takes me by surprise and I lay in our four poster bed clutching my photo of Amélie sobbing myself to sleep.

But the next morning was the start of another day and off we went to Dieppe for a coffee and a potter. As we walked around the cathedral, I panicked as we'd left Amélie in the car and I was petrified someone may steal the car with her in it. So I dragged Martin back to an outside seat for our coffee within view of the car and vowed to take her everywhere with us for the rest of the trip. I'm sure if people knew what was in our rucksack they might well think I was barking mad, but it was important to us both to have her with us on that holiday at all times.

We stopped for lunch in Rouen and there was a heavily pregnant woman at the table immediately next to us, stroking her bump as I had done so often with Amélie. I longed to be pregnant again and immersed in that unbeatable feeling of pride and impending motherhood, and temporarily put aside my sheer fear at 40 long weeks of worry and concern. I was convinced not to let it become the focus of our lives though, which we've managed successfully since Amélie died. I am glad that Martin and I are both convinced that we are destined to have a family one day, and I look forward to the day that happens.

Our next home on that trip was in a little village called Crépon, very close to the beaches of the Normandy Landings that Martin was keen to visit. It was a stunning manor house owned by the local mayor, a lovely woman called Madame Poisson. Our fellow guests were American, and I was impressed that the only one we met spoke good French. I'm really sorry now that I never knew her name, as she and I had a long conversation over breakfast. Inevitably she asked me what I did and I told her and admitted to the fact I was on maternity leave, bravely inviting the inevitable questions of "What did you have?" etc. etc . I burst into tears as I told her we'd had Amélie but that she'd died 10 weeks previously. She reacted with tears in her eyes as she told me her daughter had miscarried early in pregnancy, but now has a lively little girl they're all very proud of. Sadly everyone has a tragic story to tell if given the right opportunity and environment.

I started thinking about the marked differences in people's grief and how crucial it is to respect that everyone grieves different, so not to rush them or dictate exactly how they behave. I decided to write down the poems I'd had brewing in my head for some weeks and felt pleased that since mentally writing them I had actually progressed from my dark and suicidal depression:

Grief is dreadful, grief is grim
Grief an overwhelming din
It shuts out happiness and light
And makes each day a daily fight

Each of us differs in how we grieve
We all seem to search for some vague reprieve
From the pain and the anger, the panic and fear
The skewered heart, the loss severe

Because we're all different we need to reflect
And treat one another with mutual respect
For grief there <u>are</u> no rules or guidelines
And life carries on, with you on the sidelines........

....

I used to be strong but now I'm weak
The future was bright and now it's bleak
I used to be a mother and now I'm not
My motherhood that time forgot
I used to enjoy life and sharing and giving
And now I feel like I'm playing at living.

Re-reading these poems, I am grateful that I somehow managed to heave myself out of the depths of gloom and re-establish some semblance of normality and vague happiness. We headed for Bayeux to have a look at the tapestry and were next to an English family as we walked round the explanatory story before viewing the tapestry itself. The mother was snapping at her children's questions and requests and I promised to be the most patient mother in the world whenever our wish came true in the future. It made me sad to think that we may have had to wait until Amélie was asleep to walk round the exhibition so that she didn't disturb anyone. She certainly wouldn't ever disturb anyone now, not that she ever did during her little life either sadly. I didn't really concentrate on the story of the tapestry itself, although it was very professionally done, and instead wondered what she would have sounded like if she had ever made any noise.

I'll never know.

Baguettes And Barbeques

Dunk and Coolie called to say they'd set off late, so could we arrive at Plessala at around 4 o'clock. So at 4 o'clock we were in the only bar in Plessala having a beer in the sun, excitedly waiting for Dunk to meet us and lead the way to their French home. He appeared over the other side of the square, holding Olly's hand and pointing to where we were sitting. As soon as he saw us, Olly skipped towards us both grinning, and wondering which of our open arms to leap into. He always goes to Martin first then wants to sit with me, so he hopped onto my lap and drank the coke I'd bought to counter the fact he'd been carsick about four times on their journey. He was over-excited and chatted about their house incessantly and the fact that we'd go to the beach, play pooh sticks at the river, have a barbeque, sleep in the hammock and just "have fun Saz!". I knew we would.

Our five days with Dunk, Coolie and the kids were blissful. We talked about Amélie, and it was lovely for me to go for a bike ride with my not so little younger brother and talk just the two of us, which we rarely get the chance to do now face-to-face as our respective partners are usually there. Thankfully we all get on famously and I think of Coolie as the sister I never had, but I did feel the need to chat to Dunk on my own, so cherished the time we spent together. We took an unexpected wrong turn and had to cycle straight through a river, so soaked ourselves and cracked up laughing. There's something irreplaceable, treasured and unequivocal about the sibling bond between us, and the older I become, the more I realise and appreciate how rare our close relationship is.

We had a barbeque in the orchard on our first evening and it seemed ages since my sadness on the ferry over, as we'd very much relaxed into being on holiday. We walked down to the river to play pooh sticks from the bridge that is their French equivalent of our bridge at home in Scotland and I felt genuinely happy. However, as happens so frequently now, I was metaphorically punched in the stomach again walking behind Dunk and Martin. Dunk had Rosie in her rucksack on his back who was shouting loudly as usual in her attempts to talk, and Martin was carrying Amélie in her rucksack, our precious little box of ashes. I yearned for her to be alive and with us.

Dunk suggested we do something symbolic at their house in France in Amélie's memory, as we were all painfully aware that she should have been with us on that holiday. In the garden wall outside the house is a stone in which the names and dates of the previous owners has been engraved. Martin and I separately decided it would be an appropriate reminder to have a stone engraved for Amélie to put at the other end of the garden wall, as long as it didn't look like a gravestone. I'll investigate stonemasons online when I'm back home.

It saddened me throughout that holiday that Olly kept referring to Dunk and Martin as "the Daddies", which for him was perfectly normal, as was the fact that Martin was

Amélie's Daddy but that she was dead. I'd love to have the innocence and acceptance of a 3 year old sometimes.

On our last evening I was hit with a wave. I knew it was looming so took myself outside to sit in the garden. I got Amélie out to have a look at her and remember our precious daughter. Dunk presumably saw my shaking shoulders and came out to join me. I showed him Amélie's urn, having forgotten that he had been given a selection of urns by David Lloyd to show us whenever we felt up to looking at them while we were at home in Scotland immediately after she died. Dunk thought the plaque on her urn was beautiful, although it also made him weep. I guess the pain will ease one day for us all, but it's all still so raw and surreal.

Martin and I did have a great holiday and loved spending time with the Wimbledon Speakes and each other. We both felt we were slowly learning to enjoy and appreciate things again – good food and wine, good company, exercise in the fresh air, lovely scenery and a special French home from home. Sadly that was all dashed on our return home.

Returning home to Chiswick is never easy, as it represents the house of shattered dreams where we live our daily reality and new lives. And returning home from France was particularly difficult, as the post contained more sympathy cards and a letter from the nursery with a refund for the enrolment fee we'd paid for Amélie's nursery place. It felt like a refund for her life.

Babington House

That evening I sat in Amélie's room rocking on Olly's bed with the urn in my arms, my holiday happiness having disappeared the minute I opened the letter from the nursery. It was so frustrating to have been feeling so positive and happy only an hour previously, then to have been dragged back into the depths of despair so cruelly once again. I felt as if my progress was a false hope and that I'd taken a step back in the recovery process. I felt like a human punchbag who didn't have the energy to bounce back.

The next morning I slept for longer than usual, subconsciously delaying waking up from my recurring dream, in the knowledge that I would be spending the day writing this book, which although cathartic is never relaxing. Rayne phoned to say she'd booked dinner for that weekend at Babington House while we were staying with them, and if I wanted to have a treatment to go ahead and book it. Although I said to Rayney that I may do, I knew internally that there was no way I would survive a massage at Babington House as I should have had that fateful week, without falling apart. I knew it would bring back too many memories so thought it safer to avoid it completely. I also cancelled Siobhan coming to clean, as I wanted to create a sufficiently peaceful and private environment to write without the timeline of finishing by early afternoon. As it was also a week after the 5 year anniversary of Siobhan's daughter Fiona's death, I decided it would be too emotional for either of us to deal with if we saw one another. These type of decisions allow me a level of control that makes me feel like I am coping and creating more of an acceptable new reality.

I had lunch with Steve, my boss, the Friday lunchtime before driving to Rayne and Andrew's on the Saturday. It was lovely to see Steve, who has been a friend over the years, and I was amused by his hilarious updates of how things had changed at work in the 3 months since I left for my week's holiday. I felt immensely proud as I held it together during our lunch, genuinely enjoyed Steve's company and didn't feel guilty for having a good time. So maybe I was getting somewhere after all.

That evening, Martin and I met up with some very good friends of ours who have been trying unsuccessfully for eight years to conceive. In comparison to their plight, I actually felt lucky, in that we conceived Amélie so quickly after getting married and that we had the privilege of knowing our precious daughter for the time we did. I so wished them the unrivalled joy of meeting and holding one's child for the first time. Time will tell, but I think about them continually. As I'd started on the wine at lunchtime with Steve, by the time we weaved our way home I was well and truly sozzled, but felt good about life for the first time in weeks.

Inevitably my head hurt badly as we drove to Rayne and Andrew's the following morning, so much so that we had to stop for a motorway service breakfast en route – a sure sign that I'm seriously unwell. It was lovely to see Rayney, and we immediately started talking about our respective lost daughters. Rayne was 5 months pregnant when she gave birth to their dead daughter. Andrew cried when he hugged me, knowing the pain of losing the most precious gift on earth, and willing it to be better for us. Louis and Ben soon bounded in to the kitchen and broke the pain veneer. They were good fun all weekend, although I found it difficult not to fall apart completely when Louis asked "Saz – you had a baby in your tummy before. Where is she?" And "When's she coming back?" in response to my explanation that she's in the stars. God it hurts.

Unsurprisingly our fabulous dinner at Babington House turned into an alcoholic marathon, culminating in some home-made cocktails from Martin. All four of us howled in their garden, fuelled by our collective pain and half our bodyweight in wine. Although phenomenally painful, that release of hurt and anguish with the only friends of ours who could completely understand what we were experiencing, was a real watershed for us both in the grieving process. We wept together for our lost daughters, our shattered dreams and the unfairness of it all. Rayney reassured me that the arrivals of Louis and Ben had finally made her (five years on) look back on their daughter Georgia Lily fondly rather than with regret and pain. I genuinely hoped one day I would be able to just focus on the special times we enjoyed with Amélie, rather than thinking of her loss as an irreplaceable gap in our lives. I do feel very privileged to have been her Mummy and hope that one day soon I'll stop dreaming about her every night and instead wake every morning looking forward to whatever the future holds rather than in bitter disappointment.

Rayney wept as I showed her the photo album I now know inside out. It makes me weep less now as I've shared her more frequently, but I forget that for people seeing the awfulness of our situation for the first time – all the tubes and her incubator in the SCBU, Amélie with only the ventilator in before we embarked on the death march upstairs, the beautiful family portraits just before she died –it IS shocking and tragic. Sadly, it's part of our lives now and forever. "Oh Saz, I just don't know what to say. She's beautiful." of course fuelled my silent tears.

We arrived home from Rayney and Andrew feeling absolutely drained and exhausted – physically from our drinking marathon, and emotionally from our outpourings over the weekend. But in some way it helped, and symbolised a major hurdle in our grieving process.

I went to see my friend Al the following day who lives in a village in Buckinghamshire and braved the process once again. Complicated tears at seeing one another again for the first time, visible pain at the photo album, the explanation of our tragic story and the questions about my subsequent emotions and views for the future. As I was only about three miles away from my dear sister-in-law Coolie's parents, I decided to bite the bullet and call to see if they were around. I'd decided it would be far easier seeing them when none of us had any prior warning and therefore the dreaded anticipation of meeting again for the first time since it all began. Diana had written us some wonderful letters and I was painfully aware of the effect it had also had on Adrian, as they now consider us to be part of their family. And as parents of Coolie, they would inevitably have considered how she may have felt had they lost their own granddaughter.

I'm glad I went without Martin. It gave Adrian the chance to show his own emotions too whilst pouring over the photos of our Little Lady. Diana kept apologising for crying, and I think felt embarrassed that she was far more upset than I appeared to be. I've come a long way in the past few weeks in being able to share our precious Amélie and be supportive to others who feel our pain. We talked about our time in France the previous week with Dunk, Coolie and their gorgeous grandchildren Olly and Rosie, which sadly gave us all the unspoken connection that they would grow up without their little cousin. I'm becoming accustomed to the many associations now though and, although the pain still skewers me when I'm least expecting it, it is slowly beginning to lessen. I can look back to my suicidal wave a few weeks ago and have no comprehension of how I could ever have sunk so low into the abyss of hopeless loss and depression.

Hey Jude

I had to really psyche myself up to call Jude, Jamie's friend who lost her son Jack to cot death while I was pregnant with Amélie. I was almost glad that she didn't answer and instead I could leave a message suggesting we meet. I had looked forward to meeting her at some point, as she would fully understand my feelings of guilt, anger, bitterness, resentment and loss. She sent me a text message back. She knew the rules.

I'm seeing her on Friday and suspect it might be the beginning of a life-long friendship between us.

She was shorter and slimmer than I imagined – a tiny Irish energy ball who met me at the door with a tentative grin. I gave her a huge hug to set the rules for the foundation of the day and our friendship. I'd bought a huge bunch of flowers, and a bottle of rosé bubbly which went straight into the fridge for us to drink. I was pleased that she hadn't even started on the lasagne planned for lunch and instead we sat in the garden and talked as if we'd known each other for years. There's a very strong bond between similar women, particularly those who share a pain thankfully unknown to most. The bond between us was evident and similarities somewhat spooky: we have almost identical job functions; both have bubbly personalities and an abhorrence of "girlie women"; both love the outdoors and sport; both big socialites whose friends are more than just important to us, and so the list goes on.......

I asked her a lot about Jack, in the full knowledge that she hadn't really spoken about him since he died 7 months ago. In my mind, her situation was far worse – waking up with Jack beside her in bed, and rolling him over to see the dreaded and unexpected......... having the crash team work on her precious baby to no avail, and kicking herself that she immediately became so hysterical she didn't try to revive him herself. She has regrets. She didn't hold him after he died. She didn't have a chance to say Goodbye.

I saw his funeral service. She'd also chosen *"Over The Rainbow"*, so that cemented our unity unquestionably for good. Unlike us, they had a religious service and burial, so at least she has the solace of a place to visit. She described visiting Jack's grave since, and crumpling in a sobbing mess at the untidy state of it, whilst her 2 year old son Archie rubbed her back, saying "Mummy sad. Mummy sad." over and over again. God I felt her pain.

And yet she felt the same about our situation, having to play God with Amélie's life, watching her die in our arms, enduring the emotional rollercoaster of our time with her in the SCBU. She admitted she'd been envious of me, believing me to have a reason for Amélie's death, and took great comfort in the fact that, in so many ways, our situations were identical – neither of us had a reason for our babies' deaths, both of us had experienced the same emotions since, we both felt very tentative about planning anything for the future. Unlike Jude, I was glad I had been given the "luxury" of having time to grieve alone before facing friends and extended family – poor Jude was immediately thrown into family en masse from both sides and allowed no solitude.

Jude has tackled one major hurdle I have chosen to avoid to date. She's returned to work. In some ways I envy her level of renewed normality, but I guess if I worked for a company with around twenty employees, I too would be ready to return to the comfort of an extended support base. But with around 350 employees at VNU in my building alone, all of whom know about our sorry situation, I need even more strength than I've managed to muster so far to walk into the building and be faced with the barrage of questions, sympathy, avoidance, and the many other reactions we are now so accustomed to. As and when I do return, should I chose to, I just want to get on with my job. But instead I'll be greeted by Harry the security guard before I even get into the lift to my floor, whose story of his daughter's birth I know inside out; in HR where they responded with such phenomenal support on hearing our news; payroll, where Jenny has written some lovely notes on the payslips that have had to be sent home since my unexpected departure; editorial, with whom I've worked on many projects; research, who are my allies and sounding board for the many client proposals we bandy around; and then there are all my sales colleagues and friends, some of whom I've known and worked with in various companies for over a decade.

Whether by asking about or avoiding the subject, they will be acknowledging it, but I've now reconciled myself with the fact that if, ultimately, I chose not to return, I no longer see it as a failing. I'm not the same person I was before Amélie was born, and this may be my chance to channel my energies into a different area that enables others to benefit from our learnings.

Jude and I share something that created an indestructible bond between us that afternoon. We made lasagne together, drank our way through the rosé and some additional bottles of white and talked incessantly about our respective lost babies. There was no unease in the silences either. It gave us both a chance to reflect, and there's an unspoken respect between frank, like-minded women in our situation.

If any good could possibly come out of our ordeal with Amélie, it's the new friendships that have been created – Katie and Laurence in Mull, whom we're seeing again tomorrow, and my friendship with Jude, whom I'm seeing again next weekend. It's changed me and Martin irrevocably, but the indestructible marriage we have is, if anything, even stronger, as are we as people.

The past few weeks have been a real turning point for me. It's almost three months since our Little Lady died and I feel much stronger. I can talk about Amélie without falling apart. I still think about her all the time, but now with much more fondness and pride than pure unadulterated pain. I talk to her if we're alone in the house, and still take her with me if we go away for a few days. I feel privileged to be her Mummy and relish the photos I can pour over. The DVD will always upset me, as I yearn to have my little girl back as she is on film – alive and breathing, albeit on a machine.

She will always be our beautiful, precious baby, will always be our first-born child, will always be Olly and Rosie's cousin. She'll be with us in our hearts forever.

It wasn't supposed to be like this.

I had it all planned perfectly.

And then it started....................... waves of nauseous light-headedness, hot flushes, slightly greasier skin than normal........................

I wonder what the future holds.

Ode To Amélie

My heart cries out in agony
Just knowing you're not there
The aching pain increasing still
The ill beyond repair

I held you close and cherished
Our eleven special days
It hurts so much to know
That you're now beyond my gaze

My mother's love, my precious girl
Will never disappear
I hope the pain will lessen though
Each week, each month, each year

Amélie, my first-born child
A wriggler in the womb
Your problems' cause we'll never know
Our lives it does consume

A wanted child, intended
Our product born of love
You'll always be a part of us
Now in the stars above.

Part Two

Words Don't Come Easy

Knowing that our friends, family and colleagues were thinking of us throughout our horrific ordeal with Amélie was of great comfort to us both, whether by text, card, letter, or gesture of a different sort. I found it unbelievably difficult to speak to people directly while it was all happening and immediately after, as the slightest thing could and still can make me sob uncontrollably. I don't like putting anyone in that embarrassing situation of not knowing what to do by falling apart any more than I can help, so often find it easier to avoid verbal contact outside my inner circle.

I would however like to share the thoughts that were written by so many of the amazing people who were there for us from afar, so we can all re-read them. Some wonderfully appropriate, some struggling to know what to say, but all with an underlying message that was invaluable – that they were thinking of us. Depending on my mood, I find them of comfort or as the catalyst for the agonising pain I never thought could exist – both I'm sure are in some way therapeutic; but my main emotion is that of feeling completely overwhelmed by the phenomenal response by those dear to us to our awful situation.

The letter from my cousin Kate is already crumpled and the ink tear-stained as I have read and re-read it time and again – perfect. Rayne's letter destroys me every time I read it – at least we had the privilege of knowing our little girl.

My unexpected birth partner Srirat also conveyed with eloquence her part of this sad story beautifully. Pam's card continues to make me weep, and Saskia's continued caring support from abroad incomparable.

I feel truly honoured to have these people as friends and family, and empathise with the challenge they faced in corresponding with us. I can never repay the friends, colleagues and relatives that kept us going from afar with their messages of love, hope and faith for Amélie. The flowers, few phone conversations and many messages were a source of mental strength to us both and will be always:

Adam

Dear Sarah and Martin,
This is probably the most difficult letter anyone can write
—with an adult, as when my mother died, people write about
the character, successes and even faults of the deceased, but
with little Amélie none of that is possible.
There is only the potential of what might have been.
But be strong together and have faith that one day,
hopefully soon, you will be brilliant parents and all the more
loving for the tragic experience of the last few days.
Maria and I have been thinking and hoping for you.

With all our love,
Adam

Adam & Claire

Dear Sarah and Martin
Although the grief at the loss of Amélie will never go away,
one day the intensity will ease.
May that day come soon.
Our thoughts are, of course, with you,

Adam and Claire xx

Adrian Hughes (Amélie's wonderful consultant)

Dear Sarah and Martin,
I am sorry that I have not responded before now, and have to say that it has been lovely to hear from you as you have updated us on your wonderful fundraising efforts. It really is an incredible sum of money, and I know that you have had letters of thanks along the way, but I would like to add my thanks to both of you and all of your friends who have contributed so generously. You will know that this will be put to very good use, but of course you must come and see that for yourselves and it will indeed be wonderful to see you again.

I must also belatedly thank you for your gift on leaving the Unit – most appropriate and I can confirm (as you will have anticipated) that they fit in very nicely with my collection and have been worn (on display) on many occasions already.

I am not sure if you have heard personally from James, or whether you have heard his news (I would imagine you have). He is actually leaving our Unit in August, to "complete his training". Yes, I know that's quite difficult to believe, but as an Associate Specialist, the attitude from the authorities is that James is not trained despite the fact that he is already a senior clinician. Because of the considerable constraints of European Working Time Law, James feels obliged to progress to becoming a consultant and to do so he has to "complete his training". He has therefore secured a place on the Mersey Region Training Programme and hope-fully should only have to do a couple of years. However, it does mean that he is leaving our Unit and will be a huge loss. We would very much hope that we can entice him back as a consultant in the near future, but sadly there are no guarantees over this. As I think you appreciated to the full, James has been an essential lynchpin and link between the consultants and the families and babies on the Unit.

I have to say that I am always tremendously impressed by the upbeat nature of your letters. I am sure this masks a continuing deep sadness. I do hope that, along with the passage of time, you are able to make a start at coming to terms with your very sad loss and the particularly difficult time with us on the Neonatal Unit. It is always good to hear from you and I do look forward to seeing you when you are able to visit at some point in the future.

Kind regards,
Adrian Hughes
Consultant Paediatrician

Alex

Dear Martin and Sarah,

I was extremely upset to learn of your devastating loss over recent weeks and my heart goes out to you all at this difficult time. I would like to make a small contribution to the hospital as I know it means a lot to you.

I hope you manage to come to terms with this tragedy and look forward to seeing you both soon.

Thinking of you.
Yours,
Alex Crombie

Alex

Dear Speakie,

I thought you could use this for a beautiful picture of Amélie to maybe have by your bedside.

I think of you a lot, and hope that as the days go by things begin to get a little easier.

With much love as ever,
Alex xxx

Alex, Malcolm and Thomas

Dearest Speakie
 As I sit here down in Cornwall watching the waves roll in up the beach, I am finding it very difficult to find the right words to write.
 I think what I really want to say is that since we heard your news, you, Martin and little Amélie have been very much in our thoughts.
 It really is amazing how much love you can have for such a wee little baby, and all those early cuddles are so special.
 You know where we are if you would like to talk, visit or anything at all.

Big kisses, hugs and love to you all.
Alex, Malcolm and Thomas xxx
Loving thoughts are with you

To dear Speakie and Martin
 Thinking about you and sending you lots of love and hugs.

Much love
Alex, Malcolm and Thomas
xxx

Amanda and Lucas,

With Sympathy
Thinking of you At this sad time

Dear Sarah and Martin,
  So many tears shed for Amélie and the both of you.
No words equal to describing your loss.
We're thinking of you every day.

Much love,
Amanda and Lucas x

Andrew & Lucy

Dear Sarah & Martin,
  We were so very sad to hear the terrible news about Amélie. There seems very little one can say at a time like this, but we felt we had to write to let you know how sad we were on being told. We can't imagine how hard a time like this must be for you and your families, but I'm sure you're receiving a lot of support from all those around you.

With all our sympathy,
Andrew and Lucy

Ann (Mhairi's Mum)

Dear Sarah,
  No words can express what terrible sadness I feel for you and Martin on the tragic death of your little daughter Amélie. This should have been a time of great joy and happiness for you both but instead it has turned into a time of deep deep sorrow and sadness.
  It all just seems so unfair and I am sure you must constantly wonder why it should happen to you.
  I feel I am no help to you but I wanted you to know I am thinking of you and praying that you will both be given the strength to get through this. You have lots of wonderful friends and I know they will all be there for you, as will your family, to

give you help and support over the next few weeks and months.

Michael joins me in sending his love – we are both thinking of you.

Fondness and love,
Ann

Anna

Dearest Sarah and Martin,

In Amélie Charlotte's short life so many family and friends have thought of her with great love and will remember her even though they didn't get a chance to meet her.

I hope the book is helpful.

With much love,
Anna xxxx

Dearest Sarah and Martin,

I am thinking of you. I recently went to a midwifery weekend where I met an American lady who lectures around the world on bereavement. She lost her first child who was stillborn. I found her speaking very inspirational – I hope her books might be useful.

With love and I hope to see you in London sometime soon,
Anna xxxx

Anne (Schmidt)

With caring thoughts in your sorrow
Words seem so empty when hearts are so full of caring.
May you somehow feel the many loving thoughts that are
with you.

With deepest Sympathy
Sarah and Martin
So incredibly sorry to hear your sad news.
Thinking of you often.

Love
Anne

Anne and Paul

With Deepest Sympathy In Your Sad Loss
May the knowledge that others share your grief be a
comfort to you in your loss.

Dear Sarah and Martin,
Paul and I were so sorry to hear the news regarding
Amélie. Our thoughts and prayers are with you both and
your families at this time.
Thinking of you.

Lots of love,
Anne and Paul

Annie (the author and Sunday lunch provider!)

Dear Sarah,
It seems pitifully inadequate to write to you at such a
time – and I hardly know you after all – but I wanted to say

how desperately sorry I am that Amélie has died. The day you came here was so full of hope, and you were so looking forward to your "pampering" week and then, wham, everything changes. I don't suppose there are any acceptable explanations for these things and they seem intolerably cruel. I have no doubt that you probably feel you will never recover from the pain you must be going through, but maybe her short and precious little life will be a very special part of your family in the years ahead.

I hope the book helped – that part was written by my friend Meg who lost her first baby in the just the same circumstances so it comes from the heart.
I hope too that we will meet again soon.

Much love,
Annie

Beaty and Mike

Dear Saz and Martin,
We were so sorry to hear that Amélie has died. Few can have experienced such a loss and we can hardly imagine the pain you are going through.

Sarah and Duncan said Amélie's service was incredibly moving – our thoughts and love were, and still are, very much with her and you both at this time.

With much love,
Beaty and Mike

Bill and Becca

Dear Sarah and Martin,
Sorry not have written sooner. I had no idea what to say. So sorry to hear the terrible news.

I have no idea how you must both be feeling, but just wanted to let you know that we are thinking of you.

With all our love,
Bill and Becca

Birgitte

Dearest Sarah,
This is just a little something for you to fill. I know you will make the ending good.
Lots of love as much as ever if not more,

Birgitte xxx

Birgitte, George and Caspar

Dearest Sarah and Martin,
A small contribution to the memory of lovely Amélie. We will never forget her. Hope it will not be too long before we meet up, either here or there.
Lots of love to you all.

Yours,
Birgitte, George and Caspar xxx

Blythie,
I know a hug can't solve everything…
But maybe it would be a good start!
Lots of love,

Blythie
Call me if you need anything

Bobby and Rachel,

With deepest Sympathy

Saz and Martin,
You've been very much in our thoughts over the last few weeks. We cannot begin to imagine what you've been through. We can only offer you our deepest sympathies for the loss of Amélie.

We'd love to see you both when you are ready and please let us know if there is anything at all that we can do for you.

With love,
Bobby and Rachel

Browning

To Saz, Martin and Amélie
All my thoughts, love and hope at this special time.
Love,

Emma xxx

To Saz and Martin
I am honoured that you have asked me to share this special day to say farewell to your daughter Amélie.
As a true friend to you both, you know that I will be here for you in the difficult weeks and months that are to follow.

With love today and every day,
Emma xxx

Caroline

Dearest Sarah and Martin,
I just wanted you to know how much you are in my

thoughts during this devastating time for you both.

It's impossible to imagine your feelings of overwhelming loss and emptiness and sadness, and perhaps disbelief that the gift of your longed for daughter could be snatched away just at the moment when your expectations were at their highest.

Your beautiful baby Amélie will remain in the hearts of everyone who knew her and cared for her.

I hope you will find consolation in the hard months ahead from knowing that you surrounded her with all the love and devotion that she could possibly have wanted and that you could possibly have given her in her short precious life.

I am so sorry that you are suffering such a tragic loss. With much love and sympathy,

Caroline

Charlie and Jilly

Dear Sarah and Martin,

We were devastated for you both to hear about the loss of Amélie. Words cannot describe how you must be feeling. We are thinking of you both and your family at this very difficult time and hope our donation will help look after the babies.

We hope you have some special memories of your special little girl.
With love and thoughts,

Charlie and Jilly x x x

Charlotte and Mike
Thinking of you

Martin and Sarah,

Just wanted to let you know how sorry we were to hear about your loss.

Love, Charlotte and Mike xxx

Chris

With Sympathy
Caring thoughts are with you.

Martin and Sarah
Sincere condolences, Chris

Chris and Ness

We are desperately sad to hear your tragic news. To lose a baby after just a few days must be devastating beyond belief. Although difficult to accept now, time will help mend your lives. Here's to a happy future. Our thoughts and love are with you at this agonising time.

With love, Chris and Ness x

Chris and Sali

Thinking of you

Saz and Martin,

I am so so sorry for your terrible loss. I can only begin to imagine the pain of losing a child. I am thinking of you both – please let me know if there is anything at all I can do.

With love Sali

Dear Sarah and Martin,

Thinking about you both a great deal during this difficult time. Take some time out. Look to the future and draw on the support from your friends and family.

Lots of love and hugs,
Chris

Cilla, Katherine, Isabel and Tom

With sympathy
Thinking of you

Love from
Cilla, Katherine, Isabel and Tom
(Diana's sister and family)

Coolie

Dear Saz,

I am just writing to say how incredibly proud I am of you during this very sad and unfair time in your life and ours. I think you have been so brave and strong and stoical in the face of such an incomprehensible event. It still seems unbelievable that this could have happened to two such lovely and deserving people as you and Martin, but we are lucky to have met Amélie and will always remember our beautiful niece, and we will think about her more than you will ever be aware of.

With all my love and continuing thoughts,
Sarah xxx

Damiti and John

Dear Sarah and Martin,
We are so deeply sorry to hear about the tragic and very sad loss of you darling baby Amélie.
Our thoughts and prayers are with you.

With much love
From Damiti and John xxx

Dani and Ronan

Thinking of you

Dearest Sarah and Martin,
Words can't express our feelings for you at this time.
All of our thoughts are with you both.

Your friends
Dani and Ronan xx

David, Srirat, Max and Madeleine

A size so small…
A love so big…
A girl so special…
Wishing you Lots of Special Moments
With Your Baby Girl

Each precious new baby arrives
With unique gifts and needs,
But one thing they all share
Is the amazing ability
To give and receive love.

Sarah and Martin,
    Thinking of you all and waiting to celebrate the birth of Amélie Charlotte!

With our love,
David, Srirat, Max and Madeleine xxxx

So Sorry For Your Loss
It is impossible to know
The perfect thing to say right now.
Except to tell you
That you're being thought of more than ever.

Sarah and Martin,
With our love,
David, Srirat, Max and Madeleine xxxx

Dear Sarah and Martin,
    There are no words that I can write that will take away the pain of losing your darling daughter Amélie Charlotte. I only hope to offer you a small degree of comfort. You are such dear friends and you are both constantly in our thoughts.
    Sarah, I will never forget the look of love and pride on your face when you saw her for the very first time. The depth of your adoration was apparent, and, despite the huge cocktail of drugs coursing through your system, your powers of observation were as strong as ever when you remarked "She's got Martin's chin!"
    Amélie clearly inherited some of Martin's more noticeable features – her long legs, feet and ears! She also had so many of her own special features; I am sure you will never forget her smooth, soft, downy skin, the little button nose and her peachy little bottom! The contentment she felt when you held her against your skin, like a little frog, and the way she would stretch herself contentedly was obvious.

Through this difficult time, there have been some moments of light – some of which can only be attributed to Amélie being a fully fledged "Scally Baby", no two ways about it – the early use of the sunbed and the fact that you were.. "the posh bird from London with French name for 'er daughter", to be said with the nasal inflections and whine of the Scouse accent.

I will always remember the strange mixture of pride and, frankly terror at being your birthing partner. I am not sure you have a clear recollection of this, but I did encourage you to have a tummy tuck whilst you were on the table as well as a variety of discussions on the sewing up techniques…staples, ethnic chic beading….

And my dear girl, you bleed like a stuck pig, so much so, I began to fear for my sheepskin boots. The period in the recovery room when shock literally took hold of you and shook you to your very bones; and where I explored the option of radical career change to midwifery; as well as trying to use some of the oxygen tantalisingly available on tap…sadly there were rules and regulations about these things so I had to content myself with drugging you with your personal stash of morphine instead (Are you sure it's working? Click, click)

It has been our great privilege that we should have been a part of Amélie's life and I hope these memories will lessen the pain and help to sustain you.

Our door is always open to you both, call us if you need to talk, scream or just cry.

With our love and affection,
David and Srirat

Deborah,

Nothing can Compare
With the
Loss of a Child
Only those
Who have known such a tragedy
Can truly understand your sorrow…………..
Though words may be meaningless right now,
May you find some comfort in the love and concern
That surround you
From so many who deeply care.
With heartfelt sympathy

Sarah and Martin,

Words fail me except to say I feel your sorrow so deeply, as I've travelled this unbearable road myself.
It will get easier to bear every day, although your love for Amélie will be as strong today as it will be forever.

If you ever need anyone to talk to today, tomorrow or 3 years from now I'm only a phone call away.

Be good to each other through this trying time. Remember that men and women grieve differently which can be hard to understand at times.

You're in my thoughts and prayers,
Deborah xxxxx

Denise

Martin and Sarah,

I know there are no words that can explain how you both must be feeling at the moment. My heart goes out to you and your family at this sad time and hope you can find strength to support each other in this sad period.

Thinking of you,
Denise x

Dennis, Janne, Jacob, Stine and Stig

Dear Sarah and Martin,

We just want to let you know how much we have been thinking of you while you have been going through this terrible tragedy.

We know that words are only small comfort at this time and that you must be feeling devastated, but life goes on and you WILL come through this sad period in your life. There is a time for feeling sad but there is also a time for thinking of the future and all the possibilities that lie ahead. Remember – you're both so young – you have your whole life in front of you.

What has happened can't be changed, even though we wish it could be so. In the words of John Lennon "Life is what happens to you while you're busy making other plans." This is so true – things can happen suddenly, as in your case, which can turn your lives upside down.

But remember – you'll pull through – you're both strong – and the future lies ahead!

We send our sincere condolences to you both and our love.

Hope to see you sometime soon.
Lots of love,
Dennis, Janne, Jacob, Stine and Stig

Dennis, Christine and Adam

Dear Sarah and Martin,
So sorry to hear the sad news about your baby.
   Our thoughts and prayers are with you at this difficult time.
Yours in sympathy

Dennis, Christine and wee Adam

Diana and Adrian (Coolie's parents)

Dear, dear Saz and Martin,
   Just a little note to let you know that we are thinking of you and that Amélie's good progress is in our prayers. We've heard that she is absolutely beautiful.
   We and our friends are praying for you and we do believe in the power of prayer, so have courage – I know you are brave.
   Olly sends you much love and a picture of a dog.
All love and mental support if not the practical variety

From Diana and Adrian xxx

Dearest Saz and Martin,
   How can I find the words to express our sympathy and love for you both.
   Amélie did not want to open her eyes to the world, but she will know that you gave her every chance, and I am sure her spirit will go hand in hand with you both throughout all your lives.
   You have suffered the most terrible pain a mother and father can face, but , just as all things in nature follow a circular pattern, so I know that you will also most certainly experience the greatest joy from your children yet to come.

We will plant a tree for Amélie, and have chosen an Amelanchier which blossoms in early April with white flowers.

When you feel you can, please come and tell us all about her and show us her photograph.

With much love,
Diana and Adrian

Dear Saz and Martin,

It has taken me a long time to write to thank you for the lovely picture of Amélie and yourselves, and the copy of the address at the celebration of her life. I know that you have been with John and Liz and latterly have been travelling in the Western Isles, but now that you are due home I did want to you know right away how much we appreciated your letter and the enclosures.

We have cried so many times for you all. It is an absolutely beautiful picture which so clearly shows the love and closeness you were able to enjoy with Amélie, and how precious she is to you. The poem from the Pagan Book of Living and Dying is the most perfect expression of love and grief, and unbelievably moving.

You are two of my most favourite people – you have been wonderful with Olly and Rosie, and I know how dear you both are to Sarah and Duncan. How glad we are that we have a family connection with you, and how appalled we were when the sad circumstances of little Amélie's too-early start to life became apparent. We would not have you hurt for anything, and may you never be so again. You really have faced with the greatest courage the worst test life has to offer.

Amélie's tiny tree is planted in our little remembrance garden up at the field, where a gentle sunny sloping bank holds all our dear departed animals and where I plan to go when my time comes...

We hope you will come and see us and show us more pictures when you can, and in the meantime take the very greatest care of yourselves and remember that you really have now climbed the highest and loneliest mountain, and now you are on the other side better times will come.

Love from Diana and Adrian

Dunk

Saz and Mart,

Although the situation is an unfair one, you should both be proud of your daughter Amélie. She really is a cute kid who has a number of her parents' good qualities. She is a fighter, a lover of back massages, a sun worshipper and no doubt a Daddy's girl!

Now and in the future she will always be a key member of the family.

Thinking of you all.
Lots of love,
Dunk

Dunk and Sarah
Saz and Martin,

I have to say that over the past month you have both been inspirational. Times like these don't come any harder. The courage and positivity you've shown have been incredible. Amélie has very special parents.

Raising the money for Arrowe Park will undoubtedly help kids and their parents when they need all the support possible. Well done on what has already been achieved!

Lots of love,
Dunk and Sarah xx

Eileen and Bob

Words of comfort
That time may heal
Your sorrow
Words, however kind,
Cannot mend your heartache...
But those who care
And share your loss,
Wish you comfort
And peace of mind.

Dear Martin and Sarah
    Our thoughts are with you at this very sad time. Sylvia tells us that your baby daughter was beautiful. We are so sorry that her life was so short. Find comfort in each other and in your lovely families.
All our love,

Eileen and Bob xx

Emma

Dear Saz and Martin,
    Just a note to say that I have been thinking of you a lot. Sending all my love and the very best and warmest wishes to you and Amélie.

Lots and lots of love,
Emma (Pig) xxxx

Dearest Saz,
    First let me explain why I have typed this in a formal looking fashion. As you may have noticed in the past I have truly appalling handwriting and a long-ish letter would be a

nightmare for you to read in my indecipherable scrawl.

I have been thinking of you and Martin a lot in the past few weeks. I cannot, of course, really comprehend the grief you have been experiencing in this time but want you to know I am here. I am so sorry about Amélie and that you didn't get to spend the time you longed for with her.

I have seen the beautiful picture of the three of you that you sent to Sarah and Duncan. I am so glad you are celebrating the little time you did have together.

I think you two have been so brave. I really hope you are as OK as can be. Obviously nothing prepares you for situations like this but it seems you have been coping as well as anyone could.

Sarah tells me you're going on holiday. I hope the time away helps in any way it can. The problem with the written word is that it all sounds so empty. If I was there I would give you a big hug and we could talk properly.

Please let me know who I can write a cheque to for the fundraising you've been doing. I'd love to help. Anytime you want to meet up or talk then please please call me.

Thinking of you lots and loads of love,
Emma (Pig) xxxxxxxxxxxxxxxxxxxxxxxxxxxxxx

Emma

Dearest Saz,

I've started this letter so many times over the last couple of weeks, but have found it so hard to write.

One of the reasons is that it's been so hard to read – sadly, after so many years of nothing but note and minute-taking, my handwriting (even my Best, Joined-Up style) is sadly lacking after just a few words. So please understand that this is not typed out of laziness, but to help you, dear reader, try to decipher what I'm saying (or at least trying to say).

One of the other reasons that this has been so hard to write has been what has happened to you and Chooks. Such an unthinkable, unimaginable, horrific, tragic thing – how can I put it all into words without sounding flowery, or dismissive, or over-the-top?

I can't thank you enough for calling the other day: I've been so worried (nervous? Yes probably) about contacting you – even by post – and making you feel that you "should" get back to me when that's the last thing you want to do. So thank you, thank you for making the first move – sounds so selfish of me, doesn't it? Bereavement is such a delicate time – there seem to be no "rules" for getting in touch, what to say, when to just keep out of the way...........I wish I were there. Thank you too for keeping us informed, by text and also by asking Ratty to call. It was greatly appreciated – it was touching to be allowed into your world at such a personal time. I don't think we've ever felt more far away from people we love, or more helpless in their time of need.

Good grief Saz, this is a tough letter to write. Every time I even start to think about what you, Chooks and Amélie went through I fall apart. That something like this should happen to anyone is tragic...but for it to happen to such a loving, wonderful, perfect family is beyond tragic. I run out of words, I really do. So I think I'm going to stop – to say more would be to start going in circles. Just know my heart has ached for you every day since Chooks' phone call and you've never been out of my thoughts.

All the people I know that know you – my parents, Caroline (Fraz's Mum), Tara, Carolyn, Amanda, Deborah H, Mary, people at Carat Biz etc. were totally dumbfounded and appalled by the news and all send more love than I can convey on a page. Annie at Hypnobirthing was terribly saddened too – said she'd be writing to you soon. I'm sure you already know that if positive thoughts, prayers and love alone could have healed Amélie, she would have been the *healthiest baby ever.*

Now, I know you said that you want to see us sometime once you're back in London, which would be wonderful, to say the least (I think Fraz and Chooks are planning to go for a beer soon now he's back in Londres). But please know that I TOTALLY understand that you might want to steer clear of bumps and babes for a while. You need to do things at your own pace, darling, and I would hate for you to feel uncomfortable or forced into doing something you didn't really feel ready for.

Just know that I'm here for you 24/7, even if it's just at the end of pen (keyboard??) or phone line rather than in person and I won't be mildly offended if you decided that you don't want to hang out for a while. And in the meantime, if there's anything that I can do for you while you're in Jockland, just say the word.

Take your time, go at your own speed. And be gentle on yourself, mentally and physically (I know what you're like, gym queen) – healing is a physical and emotional process so go easy, OK?

Know that I love you heaps, and I'm thinking of you all the time, even if I've been a wuss in not contacting you sooner. I hope you understand that I was being reticent for (what I hope are) the right reasons – I didn't want to intrude on such a highly personal and private time.

Mahoosive hugs to you, Chooks and your families,

Em xx

Dearest Saz,

Well, once again you have blown me away with your strength and courage. I can't thank you enough for sending through the service and Ode – both things I will treasure forever. As for that perfect, beautiful photograph of the 3 of you – well words fail me. Suffice to say that we're photo frame shopping at the weekend.

I hope that you and Chooks have a wonderful time on your driving holiday and feel well rested.

Really looking forward to seeing you both soon – and in the meantime know that you're in our thoughts and our hearts.

Heaps of love and hugs,
Em x

Em, Fraz, Anne, Mike and Caroline

Dearest Saz and Chooks,
Just a note to let you know that we're all thinking of you and praying that everything is OK.
Sending you heaps of love and hugs,

Fraz, Em, Anne, Mike and Caroline xxx

With deepest sympathy
Thinking of you

Dearest Saz and Chooks,
We cannot express how saddened we all are for the both you and your families.

With all our love,
Em, Fraz, Anne, Mike and Caroline

Em

Hang In There
I know that things are tough right now
And you may feel alone
But please remember others care

And you're not on your own.
Just try to take things day by day
And anytime you need me
I'll be with you all the way.
Em xxxxxxxxxxxxx

Freddy and David

Dear Sarah and Martin

Our thoughts are with you at this terribly sad and difficult time. Your little lamb hardly had time to breathe.

We know what you must be going through. We would love to see you when you are feeling stronger.
All love

Freddy and David xxx

Gail

Thinking of you

Dearest Sarah

I am so sorry to hear of your terrible loss and that I am thinking of you both.

With love,
Gail xxx

George

Dear Sarah and Martin,
You may know that John has been keeping me in touch over the past days. If I can offer some comfort, it is to make sure you are aware that there is a world-wide network of your friends, colleagues, acquaintances (and a God uncle!) who

have you constantly in their thoughts.

When life improves – it will, it must – Julia and I look forward to seeing you again in London.

Meanwhile our best wishes and love,
George

George & Birgitte

It's a girl
Dearest Sarah & Martin,
Lots of love to your little bundle of love, as well as yourselves. Tell her we will be waiting for her in Combe. Before that we are hoping to visit you sooner rather than later.

Lots of love yet again to you all,
George and Birgitte xxx

Dearest Sarah and Martin,
Our thoughts and sympathy are with you at this very sad time…as you cherish the creation and short-lived life of your wonderful daughter Amélie.
ALL our love,

George and Birgitte xxx

George and Gillian

Dear Sarah & Martin,
We were so desperately sorry to hear of your very sad news. My own daughter (also a Sara) had a miscarriage in her first pregnancy, for no apparent reason, and was devastated – as indeed we were also.
The good news is she now has 2 lovely children. I know

Amélie will be cherished and remembered forever. Time is a great healer, and we hope this, and your "mission" on behalf of Wirral Hospital are helping you both through this very difficult time.

We've thought of you a lot since we heard and will keep in touch via your Mum and Dad, Sarah.

Very best wishes,
George and Gillian xxx

Geraldine

With deepest Sympathy
I send you so much love at this most difficult time. You are in my thoughts and in my heart,

Geraldine x

Gerard, Tug and Klara

Thinking of You

Martin,
So sorry to hear of your recent loss, my heartfelt condolences to you both. I pray that your pain will be eased soon,

With deepest sympathy,
Gerard Best Wishes,
Tug

Dear Martin, dear Sarah
I was deeply touched by your tragic loss.
Please accept my sincere condolences.
Be strong Klara

Gigi, Greg, Pam, Tash and Ive

Dearest Saz and Martin,

We, the Clarks and Ivan, want to give you both big hugs and send our deepest respect, sympathy and support wishes to you both.

You are in our thoughts constantly, as you were during the two weeks at the hospital.

We mourn the loss of Amélie Charlotte; a beautiful name indeed and an eagerly awaited new addition to the family we care about so much.

Fate in life as you know can sometimes hand out these savage blows but rarely so early in married life. We know you two will hang in there together, despite this. Of course we feel helpless to help you both.

However, we are hoping that time in Scotland will soon start to work its healing magic.

We are sending a cheque under separate cover; a contribution to your fundraising drive for the neonatal unit at the hospital.

With much love from
Gigi, Greg, Pam, Tash and Ive

Gill Donnelly

My dear Sarah and Martin,

Words seem so inadequate at a time like this, but I just wanted you to know how sad I am for you both and I wonder why, in this big plan of things, that two such lovely, caring people have so much pain to bear.

You have each other – draw strength from that.

With lot of love and prayers and a big hug, Gill xx

Ginny and Dave
At
Times
Like
This
We
Can't
Help
Remembering
How
Fragile
Life
Is…
May you
Find
Strength
In the love
Of
Family
And in
The warm embrace
Of friends.
In Deepest Sympathy

Sarah and Martin
We are thinking of you both
Ginny and Dave

Hazel and Paul

Dear Sarah and Martin,

Becky came round the other night and gave us the terrible news. I cannot imagine the pain of losing a baby and we want to extend our deepest sympathy to both of you. You must feel your lives have been ripped apart though I am sure there are really no words to express your sadness. Why it is that life sometimes with such apparent randomness turns so cruel is beyond comprehension.

I remember talking to a colleague once after he lost his son in his teens and he said "The world is changed forever by the birth of a person, which their death can never take away." And that struck me as very true though whether it provides even a crumb of comfort at a time like this I don't know.

Anyway, I don't know where you are at present, Scotland I presume, but when you get back we are around if you want to see us or come round or talk about it even tough I can well understand if you don't feel like seeing many people at the moment.

We didn't want you to think that we didn't know, or felt we ought to avoid the subject.

With all our love for now,
Hazel and Paul

Heather and John

Wishing you peace
In this time of sorrow

To Sarah and Martin
So very sorry to hear about Amélie Charlotte. It must be so tragic for you. It is really hard to know what to say at this very sad time, but hope that each day will ease the pain that you have endured.

Love, Heather and John xx

Hughesy and Rachel

Dear Martin & Sarah,

We are so terribly sorry about your loss. You have our love and deepest sympathy. If there is absolutely anything that we can do to help ease the pain in the weeks & months to come, we are here for you.

Our thoughts are with you and our hearts go out to you.

Hughesy and Rach

Imogen

Dear Sarah,

I was so sorry to hear about your daughter, and while I'm struggling to find something to say that isn't hopelessly inadequate, I wanted you to know that you're very much in my thoughts.

With love, Imogen

Isobel

Dear Sarah and Martin,

I write to say how desperately saddened we are at the death of your baby daughter.

I write, but without the words which might give comfort at such a painful time. Know, at least, that we are thinking of you.

With love and sadness,
Isobel

Jacob

Dear Sarah and Martin,

I'm so sorry to hear about your baby. I hope you will be able to get through this tragedy in the best possible way.

Here's a CD with that song you really liked Sarah. Maybe it will bring you some comfort – I think of it as a very optimistic song anyway.

Take care of each other and best wishes!
Love, Jacob

Jamie and Gabi

Dear Sarah and Martin,

Gabi and I were so sorry to hear about your baby. You poor things – I can't imagine how you must feel. Some very close friends of our lost a baby in similar circumstances just over a year ago and then happily had a baby a week ago, who is doing very well. They are a great couple and if you wanted to speak to someone who can share their experiences they would be very happy to hear from you. I've mentioned to them you may call, but no obligation on your part.

Our deepest sympathies and lots of love
Jamie and Gabi x

Jamie, Julie and Lily

Martin and Sarah
Our thoughts are with you and baby Amélie at this difficult time.

Lots of love and best wishes
Jamie, Julie and Lily xxx

Jamie and Naomi

They might not need me; but they might
I'll let my head be just in sight;
A smile as small as mine might be
Precisely their necessity
(Emily Dickinson)

We're thinking of you and are here if ever you need.
With love and thoughts,
Jamie and Naomi x

James (our dear "Associate Specialist")

Dear Sarah and Martin,

Just a short note to thank you and your friends for the generous donation. It will be going to improve the parents room on SCBU. That was the formal thank you now the bit from me.

Thanks for the present, the painting is done and the fence is up but we are hopefully moving to something that needs more work.

I hope one day to meet you with Amélie's little sister / brother as she will always watch over you, and look forward to your book.

Love and best wishes forever James

Janne

Dearest Sarah and Martin,

I would like to express my sympathy more than my English vocabulary allows me.

Wish I could hug you both.
Lots and lots of love Janne

Jenny

Thinking of you both at this time.
Love from Jenny xx

Jacquie and Deek (beautiful hand made card)

In Memory of Amélie Charlotte
Much loved, never forgotten
For Saz and Martin
In memory of Amélie

Love,
Jacquie and Deek

Dear Saz and Martin
We were so tremendously saddened to hear that your daughter Amélie died so tragically.
The loss of a person is always horrible but the loss of a child is really terrible – difficult to imagine there could be anything worse. It is so unfair and against the natural order.
The sickening realisation that things will never quite be the same again and that apparent certainties can be torn to shreds in an instant is very hard to bear and we are so very sorry that you have to face such a violent rupture.
Obviously, only you can know your pain, but we very much wanted to send our love and to share your sorrow that we did not have the chance to know Amélie and see her reach her potential.

With love,
Jacquie and Deek

James MacGlone (my English teacher from school)

Dear Sarah,

Tuesday's dreadful news shocked and saddened me deeply: little anyone says now can possibly beguile your sorrow. Yet your mother told me you had immersed yourself in words.

And you're quite right: we read poetry, prose – look at pictures, listen to music, enjoy films and theatre because of the human need to relate personal existence to others' wider experience – and, to complement our humanity by sharing insights and values of different minds.

Time will work wonders. But, you shall never forget, in your heart you shall not lose her – ever.

With all good wishes: sincerely,
James M. MacGlone

Jane, Rob, Kate and Anna

Dear Sarah,

We are so sad to hear about Amélie. I cannot imagine how you are both feeling.

We are thinking of you.

Love and prayers,

Jane, Rob, Kate and Anna

Jo (VNU European HR Director)

With sympathy

Dear Sarah and Martin,

I was so sorry to hear about the loss of your daughter, Amélie.

You are in my thoughts and prayers.

If there is anything I or the company can do for you at this very sad and difficult time, please let me know.

Thinking of you all.

With best wishes
Jo Brandl

Jo

Dear Sarah,

I'm not really sure what to say, but I wanted to write to say I was thinking of you at this dreadful time. Sometimes a kind of conspiracy of silence grows up around such awful events, and people don't know what to say – so they don't say anything....

So, thinking of you and if there is anything I can do, however small, I hope you will let me know.

Best,
Jo (Hurst)

Jo (one of Amélie's fabulous nurses)

To Sarah and Martin,

Thank you so much for the beautiful gift. It was really appreciated and so thoughtful.

If you are ever in the area please call in – it would be lovely to see you both again.

Thinking of you both.

Love,
Jo x

Jody

My dear, dear Saz and Martin
I was so saddened and shocked to hear the tragic news about little Amélie Charlotte. My heart goes out to you both and to your families in this dreadful loss.

Will be thinking of you all, especially on Wednesday. Your pain and grief will seem boundless, Saz; why these tragedies occur will be inexplicable, but I'm sure little Amélie was loved dearly for every precious second of her short life.

My heartfelt thoughts and prayers are with you all.

Love,
Jody

John and Christine

New baby girl
Sarah and Martin
Our thoughts and good wishes are so much with you at this deeply worrying time.

Love to the three of you,
John and Christine
Anna and Thomas
Uncle Frank
Xxx

Dear Sarah and Martin,
Words can't express how sad we feel at the cruel blow you are suffering. Sylvia told us that Amélie was a beautiful baby.

If it would help in any way to go to a "neutral" place our house in Padstow is at your disposal. Walks on the beach and balmy Cornish air could aid physical healing.

Please don't reply to this letter, as you will probably be inundated with communications when you need a quiet time. The need of friends and family to write to you at this time is greater than your need to receive messages.

Frank, Anna, Thomas, Bob and Rosemary who tragically lost their first grandchild, all ask to express their sadness.

Love from
John and Christine

Jotty, Jane, George, Soph and Hamish

Dearest Sarah and Martin,

We are completely shattered. What words can express how much we are feeling for you?

Thank God you have got such a lovely, loving, brilliant family.

We have been thinking about you SO much this week and this comes with such a lot of love from all of us.

Keep strong and if you feel like dropping in, we are home and would love to see you.

Big hugs and lots of love to you all

From
Jotty, Jane, George, Soph and Hamish xxxxx

Julia (one of the fabulous neonatal nurses)

Dear Sarah and Martin,

Just a note to thank you very much for the lovely gift you sent me – it was very kind and thoughtful of you when you must have so much else on your minds.

You are both lovely people and I know will make wonderful parents. I do hope that the future blesses you with a brother or sister for Amélie and would love to hear when this happens.

With all good wishes,
Julia McMann xx
    P.S. Made a batch of "Amélie biscuits" an hour ago and they've all gone!!

Julie (SHO in the SCBU)

Dear Sarah and Martin,
    I have waited to write until now because I felt you needed time together as a family. I hope it doesn't upset you that I have written.
    I just wanted to say how touched I was by you all and lucky to have met you. I would have given anything to have changed the outcome. It's at times like this that the medical training feels a little pointless.
    What a beautiful baby Amélie was, and didn't she change facially in the 11 short days that we all had her.
    I wish you all the best for the future. I know each day must still be so hard.
    Anyway, I hope I haven't offended you by writing and if in the future you feel able, I would love to hear if you have more beautiful children.

Take care. Love,
Julie Grice

Julie

Thinking of you
At this difficult time
I was very sorry to hear
You have lost someone

So precious to your heart
I know words can't begin
To comfort you
At this sad time,
But please remember
How much you are cared about
And know you are being kept
In thoughts of deepest sympathy
And love.

Dear Sarah,

I have only just learned of your terrible loss of your child. I can't begin to imagine how you must be feeling; just want you to know that you have my heartfelt sympathy and understanding (my parents lost my brother as a child, and I know what they went through).

Sarah; don't be alone, should you wish to talk or need a shoulder please call me.

Please pass on my sympathies to your hubby, I'm sorry that I don't know his name, it's a long time since I have seen you!

Deepest sympathy,
Julie (Southern)

Kate, Ade and Tom

With sympathy

Dear Saz and Martin,
    Thinking of you.

Love Kate, Ade and Tom xxx

"Do not stand at my grave and weep;
I am not there. I do not sleep.
I am a thousand winds that blow,
I am the diamond glints on snow....
I am the sunlight on ripened grain,
I am the gentle autumn rain....
When you awaken in the mornings hush,
I am the swift uplifting rush
Of quiet birds in circled flight
I am the soft stars that shine at night.
Do not stand at my grave and cry;
I am not there. I did not die.
(Anon)

Kate (one of the neonatal nurses who provided me with hugs and tea!)

To Sarah and Martin
    Thank you very much for your gift and your kind words about the care Amélie received. Although her life was short, she touched a lot of our lives and we are all richer for this. It was a great privilege to know you and your family.

Love from Kate x

Kate (my cousin)

Dear Saz,
    I was so saddened to hear your news. Words cannot begin to express how you must be feeling. We are all thinking of you.
    I remember the barrage of emotions when Tom was born – all the trauma, the excitement and then the desperate heartache of giving birth and discovering all is not well. They look so small and defenceless. I had the feeling of complete

helplessness – not being able to make him well and not even being able to hold him or cuddle him properly because of all the tubes. It is only now I realise how difficult a time it was. The most important thing that can never be taken away from you, is the love that Amélie will have felt and the bond you shared.

I hope you don't mind, but I have organised for two trees to be planted in her memory in Tiny Toes Wood, part of Donkley Wood in the Northumberland National Park. I'll forward the details as soon as I receive them.

Amélie will always be a part of you and a part of your life. You are lucky to have had her as a daughter and she is lucky to have had you as her Mummy. Although the pain will never go, I hope that with time it will ease.

Saz, you are constantly in my thoughts and if you need anything at all, I'm here.

Please send my love and thoughts to Martin, and Ade would like me to send his love to you both as well.

Take care
Love, Kate xxx

Dear Saz and Martin,

Thanks so much for your letter – we've really been thinking of you – especially on April 12th. It was very special to read the service for Amélie and your poetry is beautiful. If you don't mind, it would be lovely to see a photo of her.

Enclosed is the certificate for the 2 trees planted in Tiny Toes Wood – sorry it has taken to so long to come.

We'd love to see you before you go or if it's not possible how about in NZ?
Thinking of you.

Much love,
Kate, Ade & Tom xxx

The certificate reads:
Amélie Charlotte Tewkesbury
2 native trees dedicated in
Donkley Wood, Northumberland Park
Tiny Toes Wood
In Loving Memory: From Kate, Ade and Tom
6/03/05 – 17/03/05

Katie and Laurence (our new friends from Mull!)

Dear Sarah and Martin
Thank you so much for coming to Tiroran – we have so enjoyed you being here with us.
Your official grading in our little book is definitely a "10"! Take very good care and come back soon.

With very much love,
Katie and Laurence xx

Keith

In sympathy
With Caring Thoughts
Sorry to hear about your loss,
Kindest regards to Martin,
Keith

Kelly

Nothing is more beautiful than the love
that has weathered the storms of life. (Jerome K. Jerome)

To Martin and Sarah
Thinking of you.
If you need anything please call.

Love Kelly xx
(aka Scouse)

Kerry (the lovely midwife responsible for me at Arrowe Park)

Thinking of you

To Sarah and Martin,
   Cherish the time you had with Amélie .
We wish you all the best for the future.

With love from Kerry and all the staff on Ward 52 xxx

Dear Sarah,
   Thank you so much for the gift, card and very moving letter you sent me.
   I made sure everyone who knew you, Martin and Amélie read it and I tell you there wasn't a dry eye in the house. Grown women blubbing on the ward. I'm not sure what the patients thought was going on.
   I was so touched that you took the time and effort to write to me, we were astounded to hear that you'd managed to raise so much money for our SCBU. Amélie must have really touched their hearts for them to have been so generous. I'm sure SCBU are delighted.
   The Clarins gift is very much appreciated. It smells divine. The label says it's good for slackened areas – Sarah love I'm gonna need a few more bottles! My slackened areas are beyond repair but at least I'll smell nice! All my colleagues were very jealous of my lovely pot of loveliness.

It would be really nice if you kept in touch Sarah to let me know how you are getting on. I'm sure you will go on to have a lovely, healthy and happy family and if you do have more babies please please keep me informed. You were a smashin' patient and would be more than welcome back at Arrowe Park (a bit too far for Martin to visit though).

Take good care of yourself Sarah and be happy.

With much love,
Kerry xxx
P.S. I like to think that the little baby in the top right hand corner is Amélie with her guardian angel.

Lisa (one of the fabulous nurses at Arrowe Park, whose kitchen chats and hugs will never be forgotten!)

With sympathy
With caring thoughts
In this time
Of your sad loss

Sarah and Martin,
Words can't express how sorry I am.
My thoughts are with you both.

Could you ever forget her beautiful eyes
Or the way she brightened each day
Or her face which is etched in your memories
So she's never far away
Could you ever forget those precious moments
The answer of course is never
For she was part of your lives for a brief time
But she will be part of your hearts forever.

With love, Lisa xx

Lisa and Jon

With deepest sympathy
Thinking of you

Dearest Sarah and Martin
  So terribly sorry for your loss.
We're here whenever you need us.

All our love, Lisa and Jon xxx

Lisa and Michael

Dear Sarah and Martin,
  We are thinking of you both and your beautiful precious daughter Amélie.
  All our love and hopes are with you,
Lisa and Michael

(a snowdrop card – unknowingly perfect)
"Do not stand at my grave and weep;
I am not there. I do not sleep.
I am a thousand winds that blow,
I am the diamond glints on snow....
I am the sunlight on ripened grain,
I am the gentle autumn rain....

When you awaken in the mornings hush,
I am the swift uplifting rush
Of quiet birds in circled flight
I am the soft stars that shine at night.

Do not stand at my grave and cry;
I am not there. I did not die."
(Anon)

Dear Sarah and Martin,

Our love and thoughts are with you at this tragic time. The joy that Amélie brought into your lives will always be with you.

All our love,
Lisa and Michael

Dear Sarah and Martin,

We wanted to let you both know how beautiful the service of celebration of Amélie's life was. It was a perfect tribute to her short life which was so full of love.

It was good to be able to go back to the house and talk to everyone and hear more stories of Amélie. It was so lovely to see the gorgeous photos too – we particularly love your family portrait.

It is so special to know that even in times of such sadness there can be moments of laughter and happiness. We are thinking of you both and hope to see you soon.

Love,
Lisa and Michael

Lisa

My dear Sarah,

We were so sorry to return home from the weekend to Jody's phone call and the devastating news.

It is difficult to find words adequate to express sympathy: all those hopes and dreams and preparation to be wiped out in such a cruel way. All I can say is that our thoughts are very much with you and Martin, and with all the family who were also so looking forward to having a new and happy addition.

We will keep in touch through Liz, and hope perhaps to

see you when you return to London.

With much love to you both,
Lisa

Liz and Chris,

Dear Sarah and Martin,
    We are so very sorry of hear of the loss of your Amélie. Please know that we are thinking of you all the time, and that many invisible hands are supporting you right now!

With love and sympathy,
Liz and Chris x

Lolo, Jeremy, Theo and Cosmo

Dear Sarah and Martin,
    We were all saddened to hear from Srirat that you have lost little Amélie.
    We share your sorrow and send our love.
    Our thoughts are with all three of you.

Much love, Lolo, Jeremy, Theo and Cosmo x

Louby, Daws and Ella

Speakie and Chooks,
    Thinking of you – we're here for you.

Lots and lots of love
Louby, Daws and Ella xxx

Lou

Dearest Speakie,

I spoke with Saz today and have only just heard your devastating news. I can't begin to tell you how sorry we are. Daws was as speechless as I was, we / I can't even begin to imagine what you are both going through at the moment. We just stood, held each other and looked at Ella, realising how lucky we are, and it just reminds me (like we need it, right?!) just how dicey and dangerous pregnancy and birth are – even in our age of modern technology.

There are some things that are noone's fault, and outside anyone's control – it's tragic, devastating and not fair – but that which doesn't destroy us only makes us stronger – and you are the strongest woman I know! You are very fortunate in your loving husband, incredible family and very large, loyal group of friends – and we are all here for you – please don't forget that. I am, particularly, only a letter, phone call or short flight away – and I would be there within a day if you needed me – know that.

I'm very good at big hugs, long comfortable silences and boozy "putting the world to rights" sessions (Ella is very good at strutting naked in front of a mirror in her princess hat if that helps?) as and when required. Be they in Stirling or Chiswick! I also have strong walking boots – think you might have the message – I'm here if and when you need me – just call, don't be afraid to lean.

We are thinking of you, particularly today. We send you lots and lots of love, a very big hug from me to you, and a request – please call me.

Lots of love,
Louby Lou xxxxxxxxxx

Louis and Ben (Rayne and Andrew's little people)

To Amélie
A picture of fireworks for you

With lots of love
Louis and Ben xxx

Lynne (the fabulous neonatal nurse who was with us at the end)

To Sarah and Martin,
   I would like to thank you both very much for your gift. It was a privilege to have known the 3 of you. Amélie was a very special girl with 2 special parents. I will think of you all each time I have a glass of champagne – chilled of course.

Best wishes to you both,
Lynne

Lynne (one of Amélie's fabulous neonatal nurses)

To Sarah and Martin
   Thank you so very much for the lovely present, you are both very special people. It was a great honour to have had the opportunity to care for Amélie in her short life. She will be remembered with special thoughts.

Love, Lynne Steen

Macca

Sarah and Martin,

I was very sorry to hear the news about Amélie. My thoughts are with you,

Macca

Margaret

Dear Sarah and Martin,

Just to say that I'm thinking of you both as you prepare for Amélie Charlotte's funeral, and hoping that you will be able to draw comfort from each other and from those around you, as you continue to make sense of her short life.

I also hope that as you move forward in your own lives and gradually learn to live with what has happened, you will look back on the times you shared with Amélie and will be able to appreciate and to understand the profound significance of her life in both of yours.

With lots of love,
Margaret xxx

Marge

My dear, dear Sarah and Martin,

Words cannot express my sadness. I wish and hope for all the strength you can bring to cope with this painful time.

Little Amélie sounds so sweet and beautiful! Do tell her that Auntie Marge loves her too! John said you have lots of photos – I can't wait to see them!

I send you all my love,
Marge

Dear Sarah and Martin,

What a lovely send-off for beautiful little Amélie. Mary's words were such a lovely tribute to both your little baby and your commitment to each other and your family.

Enclosed is a cheque for "your mission"!! Please keep me informed – we all wish you much success!

We are now away for a week, but I'll be in touch in April.

With all my love,
Marge

Margo and Kevin

Just a little Hug by Emily Matthews
A hug can say "I'll miss you", or "I'll be thinking of you",
It can say "You're someone special" of, best of all, "I love you"
It can soothe a hurt, or calm a fear, or cheer us when we're blue –
It almost seems a miracle all the things a hug can do!
When the sun is refusing to shine on your day and you're finding it hard to cope,
When you're seeing more rain clouds than stars in the sky and you just feel like giving up hope,
That's the time when someone comes along with a smile and a warm hug that says "It's okay – Tomorrow is coming, so don't give up now – brighter moments are soon on their way!"
Just a warm little hug and smile to cheer you,
To let you know now that there's somebody near you who cares.

Dearest Sarah and Martin,

You are both in our thoughts, take care, and don't forget we are always here for you, OK!

Tons of love,
Margo and Kevin xxxx
See you soon!!

Maria (Mims)

Dearest Sarah and Martin,

I can only imagine how much your hearts must be aching with love and hope for your dearest daughter. You are all constantly in our thoughts.

With much tear-filled love
Maria, Adam and Marcus xxx

Sarah and Martin

It's so difficult to know what to say or write. We'll be thinking of you all, especially little Amélie, on Wednesday.

It's always astonishing how our paths loop and curl and double back without rhyme or reason and slowly return, to a steady plod.

I'm pleased you'll have some time in Scotland, at home to absorb and take stock – I hope the daffodils are glowing and that the warmth of spring lets you both feel optimistic for the future.

With much love,
Maria xxx

Mark, Sally, Sam, Fin and Will

Dear Sarah and Martin,

We couldn't believe the sad news of Amélie's death. It must be a very difficult time for you and your families, but being together must have helped.

Writing letters like this is not easy, words can't soften the pain but we are thinking of you and hope you are managing to find some ways of coping with this awful situation.

Mark, unfortunately, does deal with similar situations and therefore has some insight into your grief. We were pleased to hear your care was so good. Please feel free to chat to Mark at anytime in the future if you feel it would be of help.

We know you are being well looked after – send our love to your parents. Take care.

Lots of love and deepest sympathies,
Mark, Sally, Sam, Fin and Will xx

Martin, Miné, Max

Martin and Sarah

It's rare that I find myself stuck for words – especially when there's so much welling up inside me and running around in my head – but I just can't find a succinct way of expressing my feelings and thoughts.

I do love you though, and will try to be here for you, always.

I read this following piece on the way up, and thought it fitting…

"Some people come into your life for a short time only – but they leave their footprints on your heart forever"

With love always,
Martin, Miné, Max

Mary

At this sad time
Expressing deep and heartfelt sympathy to you in your
sorrow.

Dear Sarah,
   On the day I heard about Amélie's death I went over to
the church on Kingsway and lit 3 candles – one for Amélie
and one for Martin and yourself.
   Truly, I cannot imagine what the past few days must have
been like for you and your families but please know that you
are in my thoughts and prayers.
   I really don't know what words of comfort I could give
you – there are none at times like this and heaven knows I'm
no wordsmith so I'd better sign off – please don't take time to
write back – I'm sure the last thing you need is to feel obliged
to acknowledge sympathy cards,

Mary Smith (née McCormack)

Mary (Wallace)

Dear Sarah and Martin,
   I can't even begin to tell you how sorry I am for the loss
of little Amélie. Everyone will be heart-sore for you and I
know that this is an incredibly difficult time for you. But
hold onto those lovely memories – they will be with you
always....

Thinking about you,
With love,
Mary x

Maz

My dearest Sarah and Martin,

I am so sorry about little Amélie. I have been very sad about the news. I am sure you have heard many clichés at this time, but no words will ever hope to describe how much my heart goes out to you and how much I have been thinking of you. I have been thinking of you all the time.

I am certain that little Amélie will always be with you in your sweet memories and hopeful hearts.

I wish there was something I could do or say to make things OK but I know how strong you are and I know how much love you both have. So I know good things will always come to you and little Amélie will always be in your hearts.

Call me soon.
Love,
Maz xxxx

Mhairi and Shaw

Sarah and Martin,

Just a wee note to let you all know that you are in our thoughts and prayers.

And that we are here for whatever you may need (even if it is just to talk drivel!) whenever you want.

Love you loads,
Mhairi and Shaw xxx

Although she never got the chance to leave her footprints
The impression she made will last forever.
Saz and Martin,

There are no words.
We are with you in mind and send you all our love.

Love you,
Mhairi and Shaw xx

Saz,

Hello! Thank you SO much for the parcel we received – the service for Amélie sounded lovely. And I am looking forward to seeing pictures of her – and checking out the resemblances to you and Martin!!

I hope that you are feeling well and looking forward to seeing you. If you are back down here I thought we could meet up the week of the 2nd May as we move into our new house on Friday 28th April and so have a week's holiday. I could maybe show you the house and we could do lunch / walk in the country (just because we can!) etc. let me know.

It's lovely to hear from you and please remember I am always here for you – even if it is just something daft! (probably easier for me!!)

Take care.
Love you loads,
Mhairi xxx

Min, Lox and Max

Dearest Sarah and Martin,

I've been meaning to write this letter for some time but just haven't had a quiet moment to spare. Nevertheless you have been in my thoughts every day.

Sarah, thank you very much for your letter, photo of sweet Amélie and copy of the service. I was disappointed not to be able to come up to Scotland and show my support, so it was lovely to share some of that day.

I just cannot begin to describe how sorry I am about your loss. I know that no matter how much one tries, nobody will ever be able to comprehend the amount of pain you've both been through, and are still living every day. Not wanting to tamper with a healing wound, that is all I will say; other than that I sincerely hope from the bottom of my heart, that your pain will start to ease as the days pass and that in some way, shape or form you will both find peace, at some level, eventually.

Please take care of yourselves and each other. I know your love is strong and will hold you together. Remember that we're here if you need us.

All our love,
Min, Lox and Max xxx

Mirian

Dear Sarah and Martin,
I keep thinking of you a lot.

With all my love,
Mirian

Mum

Dearest Sazzie,
Thank you so very much for the Nora Seton book, and especially for what you wrote. The book in many ways encapsulates for me what we've all been experiencing – the pain and grief of an incomprehensible loss but also, in our case, the deepening of the inseparable bonds of mother and daughter.
I'm heartbroken that the bond you formed with your perfect little daughter was so cruelly shortened to those

eleven special days. The memory of Amélie will be with all of us for the rest of our lives, but it's not enough, is it? We wanted that little lady and to watch her grow and develop. We'll none of us ever understand why our little karate kid didn't make it.

But I have nothing but enormous admiration for the way you've dealt so strongly and positively and optimistically with these terrible days and weeks, especially during the emotional rollercoaster of those traumatic days in the hospital. At least you and Martin have been united throughout in your choices and in your wish for the very best for Amélie herself. You gave her all your love and support (as did the wonderful hospital staff) and she thrived at your touch and on your milk. But it was she herself who made the final decision, and we can respect that.

These are such difficult times (the worst I've ever had all my life) but I do treasure some of the times we've spent together and some of the memories of laughter (I think back to our drinks at the Sherrifmuir, our lunch in Glasgow, our day at the beach, our swims) and I feel enormously privileged that our relationship is such that I was the one who could give you so much support here at home.

I know there'll be many bad days ahead but I also know that there'll be many good, and that, with the support of Martin and the rest of our family and your amazing friends, life will gradually improve, and I wish you both joy in each other and in the future.

You know that I'll always be here for you and I love you more than words can say.

Yours, Mum xxxxxxxxxxxxx

Monica, David and Riley Eloise

Dear Saz and Martin,

Words cannot begin to express our deepest sympathy to you after your great loss. We have heard that Amélie was absolutely beautiful and we know that she was the luckiest little girl to have been showered by so much love. You continue to be in our thoughts and prayers.

All our love,
Monica, David and Riley Eloise

Nesbitts

So sorry to hear about your little girl. We're thinking of you.

With much love,
Shaun, Jane, Helen, David and Kate

Nicki

Dear Sarah and Martin,

I don't know where to start or what to say? I can't imagine what you must be going through at this moment. I would like to explain why I didn't visit with Rob and I hope you know it's not because I don't care (completely the opposite!).

This must be such a painful & personal time for you both and felt that it would only really be immediate family that you would want around at this time. It's precious time for Sylvia and Rob to be with you all and I didn't want to intrude on that.

I have also been so upset by it that I would have been a weepy mess that would have been no help to anyone!

You are such a strong couple and whatever the outcome I

know you will get through this and draw upon your inner strength to survive. This will touch all our lives forever, and at this moment in time I cannot see any positive slant on the whole situation. Other than you've been blessed with fertility and maybe sometime in the future this may be some consolation to you, but I'm sure you don't feel that way now.

My heart goes out to you all and my thoughts are constantly with you. Please give Amélie a big kiss from her Auntie Nic.

Whatever the future holds, there is always an open house for you here in Jersey, if and when you need to get away from it all.

My prayers are with you every day.
Love to you all,
Nicki xxx

Nicki and Rob

With Deepest Sympathy
Though there are no words
However heartfelt
That can ease your sorrow
It may help to know
That those who care for you
Hold you close in thought.

Dear Sarah and Martin,

We are so sorry that we are not going to be able to join you on Wednesday. I hope you realise that although we are not there with you due to circumstances we haven't stopped thinking about you at such a sad time.

We will visit our local church tomorrow in St. Brelade and light a candle for baby Amélie.

Please pass our donation on to Wirral Hospital Trust.

Thinking of you always,
Nicki and Rob xx

Dear Sarah and Martin,
   This is the little chapel where we lit a candle for baby Amélie tonight.
   It's a lovely little chapel in a gorgeous spot, on our beautiful island.
   We look forward to taking you there when you visit us in the summer.

Lots of love,
Nicki and Rob xxx

Ninian

Dear Sarah and Martin,
   I have been wanting to send you thoughts and love to you both since John told me about your tragic loss. I am sure you have been brave throughout the ordeal and you have a lot of love and support around you, and yet it is deeply personal and extremely hard to endure.
   There is, of course, a bigger picture and only time can give us the answers as to why this should happen. But I am sure that there is a greater reason for these things than we can fathom just now. You are both wonderful people and I have wonderful memories of your wedding day. May you both be given the joy and love of children and a long and happy life together in a warm and loving family of your own.

With all best wishes and much love,
Ninian

Olly

(This is a picture of a dog)
Dear Saz and Martin
  I love you

Love from Olly xxx

Pam, Turlough and Kiera

Saz and Martin, dearest, dearest friends,
  We wanted to say how sorry we were to hear your sad, sad news... but sorry just isn't enough. Amélie's death is a tragedy. In her short life with you she was a very, very well loved little lady and she will continue to be in all our hearts, minds and thoughts in years to come.
  You know that we were thinking about you and Amélie over the past weeks. She certainly was a fighter allowing you to know her, and touching many lives.
  She was the very special daughter of a very special couple. We hope we can help in some way however small in the future and will make a donation so that Amélie's legacy lives on and helps other "little people".

Forever,
Pam, Turlough and Kiera xxx

Patrick and Karin

With sympathy
Thinking of you
Martin and Sarah
Sincere condolences,
Patrick and Karin

Paul, Gail and Simon

On The Sad Loss Of Your Daughter
This must be
A very sad time for you,
But please remember
You are never completely alone,
While you're in the thoughts
And in the hearts of those who care

Deepest Sympathy
To Martin and Sarah

With love from Paul, Gail, Simon xxxxxxx

Pauline (one of the fabulous nurses who looked after Amélie) A snowdrop card – knowingly perfect

Warm and sincere thoughts are with you at this sad time

Dear Sarah and Martin,

I don't know what to say other than I am so sorry and sad for you both now Amélie is no longer with you. Your time together was so precious and I feel honoured to have been able to care for such a beautiful baby and support the most fantastic parents. All three of you were a joy to have met and I just wish the circumstances had been different. I'm sure there must be a reason for all this heartache – surely it must make you stronger as a couple?

Amélie was only with you for a short, stressful time, but remember her with happy thoughts – how pretty she looked in her little dresses and matching knickers, and how much emotion surfaced when you cuddled her.

I'm sure it is very difficult to look forward but I honestly hope your dreams will come true soon.

Take care of each other.
All my love to both of you.

Love,
Pauline Fong x

Dear Sarah and Martin,
    Now I don't know where to start! How could you begin to think of special and appropriate gifts for the people you have met and shared Amélie's little life with? You are a remarkable and wonderful pair!
    A lot of thought has obviously gone into my present and I do appreciate it. It made me cry and laugh. Your beautifully worded card also reduced me to tears. How do you do it?
    So how's things? I guess you are still on a rollercoaster ride of emotions and I'm just so glad you are a strong couple able to cope with the tough things life throws at us.
Well, we had a great holiday. Steve took happily to the red runs by the end of the week thank God! My friend Liz married Andy halfway down a ski slope on the Thursday.
Noone knew their plans, not even her own son, only the registrar they flew up to perform the ceremony. Plenty of champagne that day! Then on our last day, I came down Pointe de Myon and fell, tearing the medial collateral ligament in my left knee. The pain was unbelievable; I ended up in a skiddo and ambulance. Still, it's not put me off.......I'm going again! I was off work for a week until I could weight-bear. Now I'm okay in a very attractive knee support with hinges. What a bummer!
    Well Sarah, I wish you all the very best for the future and hope all your dreams come true with Martin and next time you are on the Wirral (be careful!!) please ring me – I'd love to hear from you.
    Thanks again for my wonderful presents.
Love Pauline

Phyllis

Thinking of you
Dear Sarah and Martin
 I am so very sorry.
From Phyllis with love xxxxx

Rachel (one of Amélie's fabulous nurses)

Dear Sarah and Martin,
 I would like to thank you for my beautiful present and card. It was very thoughtful of you to think about all of the nursing staff and doctors and your kindness has been much appreciated. I was very grateful to have cared for Amélie for those precious 11 days as she was a beautiful little girl who touched us all. She was very lucky to have such caring parents and such a dedicated family.
 You were wonderful parents and I am sure in the future all will be well for the pair of you and Amélie will remain a precious memory. Memories last forever and she will be a beautiful angel watching over you through your grief and through your life together.
 Don't forget to come and visit us with your family in the future because it always makes our job worthwhile! I feel very privileged to have cared for Amélie and your family and I wish you all the best in the future.

Yours sincerely,
Rachel

P.S. Hopefully our Scouse sense of humour made you laugh (or larf!) through the hard times on the unit and you will cheer when Liverpool footie team score!!

Rachel, Verity and Sarah,

We're Thinking of You with Sympathy and Caring
Although we know
At such a time
There's little we can say,
We want to let you know
That you're in our thoughts each day.

Dear Sarah and Martin,

We were so sorry to hear of the loss of your daughter Amélie. Our thoughts are with you both,

Rachel, Verity and Sarah

Rayne

Dearest Saz

This blanket is just a little gift for Amélie – a bit cosier than the hospital stuff. It's been washed in the mildest of detergents and should smell nice for her. Her other pressie is here and I will send on when you bring her home. The camera and photo album is so you can show her how tiny she was as a newborn – take lots of photos… she'll grow so fast. Plus some things to make you feel more like yourself. If that's possible.

You know, Amélie could have no parents more committed and adoring of her. You and Martin will get through this one at some point. You're both fantastic people with nerves and backbones of steel. You have a fabulous family Saz and a network of friends who will bend over backwards to help and support you – the three of you.

Some days you'll wake up and wonder how this all happened and life will sometimes feel like suspended animation. But Andrew and I learnt the hard way too – and one day you wake up and just feel acceptance. You're incredibly strong-minded and she simply could not have a better mother.

But remember you can't do this by yourself, all of the time. We know that Martin, your parents and Dunc will be pillars of support, so please use them all. You're an inspiration Saz, but not infallible. Look after yourself too.

We think of you and Martin and Amélie so much. If Amélie is even a little bit like her parents she'll do everything expected of her, and then a little bit more. You know where I am – use me if you need to.

Our special love to the 3 of you.
But super-size hug to you from me,
Rayne xxx

Dearest Saz,

Thank you so much for your letter and for sending Amélie's service. So many wonderful words for clearly a much adored baby girl.

I simply can't fathom how you must feel. I hope that being at home in Scotland will give you and Martin the time and space to grieve Amélie's unfathomable passing and to start building up the strength to go back to normality, whatever that is, down south. I know that Stirling has always been your buffer zone and I'm so glad you can find the peace, quiet and undoubtedly the love and support you need.

Andrew and I have become very philosophical about Georgia Lily's death. We were lucky to have an amazing support network, from friends and family to the midwife team dropping in for a cuppa. Life was pretty low at the time, as you know. But 4 years on I look back and think – yes – it was bloody awful and indescribably painful. But I'm here, I've not lost the plot with grief. And I can still see her face, the replica of her father's, as if I saw her this morning. She taught me so much without even knowing it. Life is a chance and our children are hostages to fortune. And when you and Martin go on to have Amélie's siblings, the joy of their arrivals will be so poignant and healing.

I'm rambling. As usual. I just wanted you to know that keeping busy is great and a key way of keeping occupied. And I'm so proud of your fundraising effort. But do please give yourself the opportunity to turn the corner emotionally. If I know you at all, the urge to do something constructive out of all this will be monumental.

I've enclosed the ARC mag I got for 4 years. You might find it morbid. I was stunned that things really do happen to babies all the time – it made me feel less isolated. If it's OK by you, we've made a contribution to ARC – Amélie made me think so much about how ARC played a key role in our lives. I hope you won't mind a slightly pathetic donation as a result. My love to you both – and Liz and John too. Terrible for them to see you go through this as well as losing their beloved granddaughter. Wish I would do more to help you. If I can – name it. Huge hug honey – thinking of you every day.

Love from Rayne xxx

Rene Bamber (one of the neonatal nurses on the Unit)

Dear Sarah and Martin,

I was so sad not to see you when I returned from my break and send you my sincerest sympathy to you both and the grandparents on the loss of little Amélie.

Sarah, you were a wonderful mother, so brave, so positive and cheerful when inside you must have been in turmoil. Having the support of a loving partner and family must have helped so much. I am glad that you were *able to bury Amélie on home ground in Stirling.*

You were a lovely person to have on the Unit, unfortunately I never got to meet Martin – my anti-social hours!

Thank you so much for all the lovely treats that kept appearing and for all the super personal presents. I was delighted with the hand cream which reposes on my dressing table and is in daily use, thank you.

Amélie will always be a part of you and her brothers / sisters will I am sure arrive in due course. Good luck with all of that and in your future lives.

I do hope we'll be able to see you again one day in happier circumstances. We'll never forget you, certain people and events seem to touch and move us in a special way.

With love and best wishes,
Rene Bamber xxx
P.S. Amélie's chocolate brownie recipe has gone in my cookery file and will I am sure be enjoyed and devoured!

Rich

A Baby Girl
Just For You
Congratulations on the
Birth of your Baby Girl

Dear Martin and Saz,

Many congratulations on the birth of Amélie. I am sure she is a beautiful little girl.

Sorry to hear of any problems, but I know that as a family you will be strong.

You are all in my thoughts and prayers and I look forward to seeing little Amélie in due course.

I hope you can find time to celebrate bringing a new life

into the world – the drinks will be on me next time.

Meanwhile, please know I am thinking of you and will help in any way I can.

Your friend,
Richard Draycott

Robert and Anne

Dear Sarah,

I enclose a cheque from us for your hospital fund which I am sending you in Stirling – I hope you're still there and beginning to relax a little. I do hope you both had a lovely break this last week with some reasonable weather.

Lots of love to you both
From Robert and Anne

Rose

Just a note to say I am thinking of you all every day and to let you know there is a candle burning for you in beautiful Christchurch cathedral, NZ.

With much love,
Rose xxx

Rosemary

Thinking of you
At this sad time
Martin and Sarah

I'm so very sorry,
Rosemary

Ross and Karen
In Sympathy
Thinking of You

Dear Saz and Martin,
Lots of love
Rosco and Karen

Ruud (a snowdrop card – unknowingly perfect)
(VNU European CEO)

With deepest sympathy

Dear Sarah,
*   My deepest feelings of sympathy and my sincere*
condolences on the incredible and dramatic loss that you and
your partner had. I pray the two of you will find the strength
to cope with this,

Ruud

Sally, Nick and children

Dear Sarah and Martin,
*   Just to say how sorry we were to hear about your baby –*
we are very sad for you both. The death of a child is the most
unimaginable shock and sorrow. I hope that you are begin-
ning to feel better physically, Sarah; please let us know if we
can do anything.

Love Sally, Nick and children

Sam and Tom

Dear Sarah and Martin,

Just a wee note to say that both Tom and I are thinking of you during this horrible time. I know words never really express true feelings, but I hope the odd note from friends puts a smile on your face.

Always here to talk if you need to.

Lots of love,
Sam and Tom xx

Sarah Bradley (NCT)

Dear Sarah and Martin,

Please find enclosed a full refund from the West London Teachers Group. If there is any further support we can offer please do call me.

Kind regards,
Sarah Bradley

Sarah and Giles

Dear Sarah and Martin,

I'm not sure if you remember us — we met at Mhairi's birthday weekend away a couple of years ago.

Mhairi has told me about your very sad news. We can't imagine how you are feeling although we are trying to as we lost a baby in a miscarriage at 4 months. Not the same as your loss I know, but I understand a little.

All I needed to hear from someone at the time was that things will get better and you will come to terms with the tragedy and also that you will feel like yourselves a bit more some day.

If it helps that I've said this to you then great because it is true. Hope this makes sense. We send you our best wishes.

Regards,
Sarah and Giles Fox

Saz, Laz, Charlie and Summer

Dear Saz,

A few little goodies for you for your stay in hospital (some to share with Martin and some just for you!). Quite a lot of pink I know but I thought that a bright colour may help brighten your day!

Thinking of you all, all of the time. Please let me know if there is anything I can do to help.

We are all sending you lots of positive thoughts and tonnes of love.

All our love,
Saz, Laz, Charlie and Summer xx

Simon

Dear Sarah and Martin,

I find it impossible to find the right words to convey my thoughts at this difficult time for you.

The both of you and Amélie are very much in my thoughts and prayers.

Everyone in the office sends their warmest regards.

Best,
Simon

Siobhan

Hi Sarah and Martin,

I am so sorry to hear about the big loss of your lovely baby. Take it day by day – I know, I've been there. Hope you do get away for a few days.

Best,
Siobhan

Stephen and V

Dear Sarah and Martin,

We were so sad to hear of your loss. Our thoughts are with you... if we can help with anything please let us know.

We wish you both well & to look to happier days ahead. All our love,

Stephen and V xxx

Steve

Dearest Sarah and Martin,

It's with great sadness I write this note, my thoughts have been with you constantly through this tragic ordeal.

Amélie's short life brought joy and sorrow in equal measures, and your memories will rightly focus on the joy. Amélie is being cared for in the very best place, and will continue to bring happiness and love to those that loved her.

With the love you share, and the fond memories you have of beautiful Amélie you will take positive things from this experience and look forward to a long, close and fruitful relationship moving forward. My very deepest sympathies.

With love, Steve

Steve and Molly

With Deepest Sympathy

Dear Sarah and Family
 We were so sorry to hear about little Amélie .
 We are thinking about you all at this incredibly difficult time.

Love,
Steve and Molly

Stine, Stig and Hjalte

Dearest Sarah and Martin,
 This is probably the most difficult letter I've ever written... Actually I had just finished a letter ready to be posted, when all this with little Amélie happened.... A letter to thank you for the wonderful nightsuits and baby-grows you sent to Hjalte. It's not a bad excuse but an explanation why you haven't heard from me. I felt terrible!!!
 Our feelings are not to be compared, but we felt very strongly How could we be so lucky / happy and not you too.. I can put myself exactly in your place: feeling so much wonderful life, but the feeling of having life abruptly taken away from you must have been devastating. And the feeling of loss indescribable. Stig and I hope that time has slowly begun to heal the wounds, even if you always will feel the sorrow she will always be in your hearts of course!
 Hope it will not be too long before we see each other again – I'm still waiting for Stig to propose! We're otherwise fine, enjoying the summer watching Hjalte grow up, presently trying to crawl and find his balance. Anyway that's all for now – once again apologies for this letter taking such a long

time to be written. It just felt so unfair!! We're sure that everything will succeed for you next time. Have a fantastic summer and send everybody our love and greetings.

Lots and lots of hugs and kisses from Stine, Stig and Hjalte (who as you can see is full of happiness and charm) xxx

Sue

My dear Sarah,

Robert has told me of the loss of your baby daughter. My heart goes out to you both.

One of the cruellest blows that life can throw at you is to lose a child.

I know how hard it is after such a loss not only to recover your physical strength but to pick up the pieces and face the world without the baby who has been so eagerly awaited by you both.

However, with the love and support of your family and many friends the pain will gradually ease and you will get through the bad days. Your daughter will always be a part of you and your life although she won't be with you in person – and to talk about her and think about her will help you. Look after yourself.

With love,
Sue

Sue

Hi Sarah,

Just wanted to say how sorry I am to hear your sad news and to let you know that I'm thinking of you.
Love and best wishes
from Sue (Burnell)

Sue and Roy

Dear Sarah and Martin,

We were both very sad to hear of the loss of you baby Amélie. Our thoughts have been with you, and we send our very best wishes and love for your future,

Sue and Roy x

Susan Bennett

Congratulations
A Baby Girl

Dear Martin and Sarah
I just wanted to drop you a line to welcome Amélie into the world and to let you know we are all saying a prayer for her here in St. Andrews.

Love
Susan and all the staff at the Royal Bank of Scotland x

Suze and Scott, Nad and Sarah, Ben and Emma, and Justin

Dearest Sarah and Martin,

We are all so upset to hear of your tragic loss, and it is hard to imagine what words can offer comfort.

But we wanted to send you this card and donation to let you both know that we are all thinking of you at this very difficult time.

With all our love,
Suze and Scott, Nad and Sarah, Ben and Emma, and Justin
xx

Sylvia

My dearest Sarah,

Have just read your email with great emotion and love.

We will all come through this I know, and in the end our memories will sweeten and will be with us forever. You are I am sure getting all the concerned telephone calls and cards, all with that first question "How are you?". Well the answer has to be, in my instance, bitter and twisted, which is why I have put it down on paper.

You and Martin have always known that I had an underlying religious streak which has certainly taken a knock. John and I had a conversation on this when I was in the Wirral and I was still clinging on to my beliefs. I've wrestled with quite a few things lately. I still believe in my inner force and strength which will see me through and help my loved ones. I know my beloved granddaughter will have siblings and I can already hear the conversation I will have with them.

I take great comfort in the love and strength you and Martin have in each other. Don't be afraid to go forward - it is life's natural cycle and a tribute to our lovely lady. Let me help when you need it and take our love and support.

Beloved daughter you will have plans and they will come to bear.

My love as always,
Sylvia xxxxxxxxxxxxx

Tara and Stephen

To Martin and Sarah
Thinking of you both

Best wishes
Love
Tara and Stephen xx

Tash, Ivan, Pam, Greg and GG

Hi Saz, Hi Martin
I've enclosed a "Clark" cheque.
Lots and lots of love

Tash, Ivan, Pam, Greg and GG xxxx

Thelma

Dear Sarah and Martin,

I find it impossible to find suitable words to tell you how very sorry and sad I am to hear of the loss of Amélie. I can only imagine the pain and sorrow you've had to bear over recent days. It must be absolutely devastating to have lost your baby and not so long ago Martin's father. You've had and are having a traumatic time, but you are in such a close loving family that I know you couldn't have better support, comfort and love.

The present is very sad and dark but I'm sure there will be brighter, sunnier and happy times in the not too distant future.

I'm sorry that I can't be of any practical help to you but you are both constantly in my thoughts.
I send you my love,
Thelma

Tim and Becky

Thinking of you
To dear Sarah and Martin
   Our thoughts are with you both – please let us know if you need anything.

Love from Tim and Becky x

Tracy (lovely SHO who looked after Amélie during the long nights)

Dear Sarah and Martin,
   I did not get to speak to you before you left Liverpool, but I would just like to say that I am so sorry.
   Sometimes life seems to be without reason, but I do know that Amélie and the pair of you touched everyone who knew you on the unit. The courage and kindness you showed were remarkable and our gossip, giggles and tears at stupid o'clock in the morning are something I will never forget.
   Amélie is at peace now and I hope you can find your peace too.

Lots of love,
Tracy xxx

Trudy, Joe and family

Thinking of you
Especially at this time
And wishing you strength

To Sarah and Martin
You will be in our thoughts and prayers,
Trudy, Joe and family

Vicki

Dear Sarah and Martin,

I am so, so saddened by Amélie's death and cannot imagine how terribly emotional it must be for you both and your families. I am at a loss to know what to write, but I want you to know my thoughts have been and remain with you.

With love,
Vicki xxx

Yvonne Simmonds

Thinking of you at this very sad time.

Sarah,

We were very sorry to hear of the loss of Amélie. We understand you are going to Scotland for a few days. We would be happy to visit you and support you at this time if you would like. Please please call us,

Yvonne Simmonds (Health Visiting Team, Chiswick)

Sands leaflet "Saying Goodbye To Your Baby"

Slowly things will change until you can carry your memory of your baby and your sadness, and it no longer carries you.

We will read these for comfort and the memories for a very long time to come.

I wonder what the future holds.

Epilogue

THE SUN WAS shining the day that Amélie's brother Joshua Harrison was born on February 24th, 2006, a mere fortnight prior to what should have been his sister's first birthday. My pregnancy with Josh was an emotional rollercoaster of fear, denial, anticipation and dread, masked by a veneer of joy and trepidation in the rare moments when I dared allow myself to believe the pregnancy might actually result in a live, healthy baby. I prepared for his birth by trying everything in my power to encourage the little lad to arrive into the world naturally, and have since lost all faith in any of the old wives' tales I took great stock in adhering to during the latter stages of my pregnancy with him. I now believe that babies are born when they're ready to be born! (At least in those instances where, unlike Amélie, there are no complications and no unnecessary intervention.) Whether sex, raspberry leaf tea, reflexology, long, brisk walks, spicy foods (I had my first and last vindaloo once I'd gone past his due date…),or fresh pineapple, I can now categorically state that, in my case, none of it worked.

As with Amélie, I had a very healthy pregnancy with Josh, who kicked at exactly the same regular intervals in the womb that his sister had. It was a source of combined comfort and angst for me, to know that my little man (I instinctively knew he was a boy from very early on – Martin now thinks I'm a witch!) was kicking and healthy, but each karate kid move was a painful reminder of our Little Lady's earlier movements before it all went so horribly wrong.

A week after his due date passing uneventfully, I had a consultant appointment at Queen Charlotte's, where

Amélie should have been born, and was given the news that, given the fact we had no actual reason for Amélie's demise and subsequent death, they believed it would be more sensible medically to embark on another C-section 2 days later. I felt remarkably calm at the prospect – I suppose partially as I knew exactly what to expect, and partially as I was crawling the walls with impatience and eagerness to meet my son. I was also petrified as to how I might react at holding a baby who could make snuffly noises, feed, and do all the things I had so desperately hoped for his older sister.

Back in control, I was able to plan our last 2 days together as a couple. Martin took the time off work and we spent both glorious days talking about Amélie, imagining potential similarities between our two children, sharing our concerns and walking round Kew Gardens, daring for the first time to visualise family life with a living baby. That said, although we had managed to resurrect the cot, the only other baby items I had felt able to retrieve from the storage bags were sufficient babygros, the car seat and maternity bits and pieces for me that I needed to pack for hospital.

Martin questioned the accuracy of the heart monitor when I was so calm in the operating theatre but of course, unlike me, he was living the experience for the first time. By that stage, as Josh was booting my stomach so hard that all the medical staff could see it form the outside as much as I could feel him internally, I felt confident that all would be well with our son's health – although I feared how I might feel when he actually appeared.

There was a radio on in theatre and everyone, including me, was singing along to the familiar songs accompanying Josh's arrival. His head appearing was accompanied by the James Blunt song *"You're Beautiful"*, which will remain an (over-)emotional favourite for me for a long time to come. And by God did he let us all know he'd arrived in the world….. he let out a yell that reassured me this chunky male version of his sister would be fine, thank you very much.

I still have awful days when I ache to have enjoyed with Amélie what I have been privileged to delight in with Josh – normal breastfeeding, first smile, first tooth, first wobbly steps, first words (I wept for quite some time the first time he said "Mummy"). Although we don't compare our two children, there are some obvious similarities that are impossible to escape – big feet, the smoothest skin imaginable, tiny downy hairs on their long backs, Martin's ears, and beautiful midnight blue eyes. Josh has got my chin though, unlike his sister. Our little blond bombshell is nearly two now and a delightful, chatty, entertaining little boy, who kisses his sister's photo every morning and is learning to say her name. I relish my every second with him, and feel proud to have produced two such beautiful children, even if one is no longer with us. That said, there are days when the reminder I see in Josh is too much and too painful and I just have to walk away from him temporarily.

We've both successfully tackled many hurdles though since our Little Lady decided she'd had enough of fighting against the cruel blow she'd inexplicably been dealt – I'm back at work full-time; have worked to counsel many other bereaved Mums; can now cope with insensitive questions and comments far better; and feel proud to have survived a horrific experience, without it ruining our marriage or my sanity (friends and colleagues, and especially family may well question that claim of course!). Having been at the depths of despair and seriously contemplated suicide, I'm now far more empathetic towards those who have genuinely suffered true tragedies; and far less tolerant of those who whinge about the most trivial issues that, in my new world of re-defined priorities, seem laughable.

I've lost some friends, and gained invaluable new ones throughout this journey. I now feel I know who I am and what's important to me. And I hope being Amélie's Mum has made me a better person in some way. She certainly gave me the pride and adoration fitting of any beautiful child that I now also pour into Josh.

People's reactions still amaze and appal me. Even those who said and wrote loving, supportive words after Amélie died seem to have almost forgotten the pain we endured, and make highly inaccurate assumptions that, because we've successfully had another healthy child since, our pain at losing our first child had disappeared. How wrong they are – one would never assume if someone's best friend or spouse had died, that by suggesting they were replaceable would be acceptable in any way, yet because noone knows how to react to the death of a child, there is much education to be done.

I still see danger for Josh everywhere I look; although agreeing to our family portrait being used to raise national awareness for Sands, I find it traumatic seeing our photo on the homepage of their website; and I wonder what Amélie would have been like, had she survived.

And I'm currently expecting our third child. The emotional rollercoaster lives on daily, and I have no idea what the future holds................

I do know though, that I'm a survivor, and the proud mother of two very beautiful children.

Sands
Stillbirth & neonatal death charity

In the UK, 17 babies a day are stillborn or die within the first twenty eight days of life; a devastating bereavement for the parents and for their families and friends.

What we do

Sands is a national charity, established by bereaved parents in 1981.

Sands core aims are to:

- Support anyone affected by the death of a baby.

- Improve the quality of care and services bereaved families receive from health professionals following the death of their baby.

- Promote research and changes in practice that could help to reduce the loss of babies' lives.

Sands head office:
Open: 10am-5pm,
Monday to Friday
28 Portland Place
London
W1B 1LY

Helpline: 020 7436 5881
Office: 020 7436 7940
Fax: 020 7436 3715
E mail:
support@uk-sands.org
Website: www.uk-sands.org